What readers are saying about
The Velvet Rage

"What a great book! I felt as if a window had been opened to the hearts of so many people I have known and loved in my life."—**Joey**

"As I read [*The Velvet Rage*], I kept bumping into myself and, hopefully, my former self. . . . I felt that [this book was] talking specifically to me and I'm sure all gay readers will have the same reaction."—**Thomas**

"Alan Downs has opened the door to the heart of every gay friend I have ever known. As a 76-year-old straight woman, for the first time I feel I have a better understanding of the gay life. Anyone who has ever dealt with or is dealing with shame will benefit from this book."—**Katherine**

"This isn't just a social commentary or self-help book aimed at a minority population. Every reader will learn from a journey through cultural values about human flaws and perfection to arrive at a place where real and authentic human hope may be found."—**Karen**

"My partner and I have read [*The Velvet Rage*] twice, and I really think it has changed our lives. Sometimes, we'll read a page or two to each other out loud just to remind us of what we've learned."—**John**

"*The Velvet Rage* is a book that will help so many people, those who are gay and those who are not. I admire [the author's] ability to write in a casual style that reads with depth, warmth, and humanity."—**Jeff**

"This book should be a 'must read' for any gay man who is committed to becoming his absolute best self in an increasingly crazy world."—**Steven**

"[Dr. Downs] hasn't pathologized homosexuality. He's described, with eloquence and intelligence, the natural consequences of what amounts to soul murder."—**Barbara**

"This book offers a human perspective on how American culture affects gay men in the twenty-first century. As a clinical social worker, I was moved by the vulnerability Downs allows himself by sharing some of his own life story, ideas, and experiences."—**Beth**

THE VELVET RAGE

THE VELVET RAGE

Overcoming the Pain

of Growing Up Gay in

a Straight Man's World

COMPLETELY REVISED AND UPDATED SECOND EDITION

ALAN DOWNS, PH.D.

hachette
BOOKS

New York

Cataloging-in-Publication data for this book is available from the Library of Congress.
Previously published by Da Capo Lifelong 2012
First Hachette Go edition: 2020
ISBN 978-0-7382-1567-9 (paperback)
ISBN 978-0-7382-1585-3 (e-book)
Library of Congress Control Number 2012933548

Hachette Go, an imprint of Hachette Books
Hachette Book Group
1290 Avenue of the Americas
New York, NY 10104
HachetteGo.com
Facebook.com/HachetteGo
Instagram.com/HachetteGo

Hachette Books is a division of Hachette Book Group, Inc.
The Hachette Go and Hachette Books name and logos are trademarks of Hachette Book Group, Inc.
The publisher is not responsible for websites (or their content) that are not owned by the publisher.

Note: The information in this book is true and complete to the best of our knowledge. This book is intended only as an informative guide for those wishing to know more about health issues. In no way is this book intended to replace, countermand, or conflict with the advice given to you by your own physician. The ultimate decision concerning care should be made between you and your doctor. We strongly recommend you follow his or her advice. Information in this book is general and is offered with no guarantees on the part of the authors or Hachette Go. The authors and publisher disclaim all liability in connection with the use of this book.

LSC-C

25 24 23 22 21

Dedicated to
Blake Hunter and Bob Ward
*May I grow as young in spirit, as wise in life,
and as steadfast in love as you.*

Contents

Preface to the 2012 Edition

It's now late August and another summer is quickly slipping away. I'm sitting on the patio in front of the weather-worn, shingle-clad cottage that my good friend, Randy, has rented for the summer in Provincetown, Massachusetts, where every summer evening he gives an entertainingly realistic performance as Cher to eager sun-drenched and alcohol-infused crowds. As the noon sun is peaking just overhead now, my heart is full of gratitude, for I've been so lucky in life. Good friends, work that I love and am passionate about, and—not the least—I am alive. Next year I will cross the half-century mark, and my mind wanders back through all those winding corridors of years in San Francisco, New Orleans, Key West, and New York. I remember all those beautiful masculine faces that grace the walls of my memory. Some didn't survive the AIDS crisis, and countless others didn't survive the angst of knowing they wouldn't die, that HIV was a chronic, manageable illness, and so they dove deep into the darkness of crystal meth, alcohol, and the like, dancing their way into the arms of death. Just last night came word to Randy that yet another old friend had drunk himself out of existence. I, like so many gay men, have savored the highs and trudged through the lowest of lows in life—and we are truly fortunate to have survived when so many others did not. At moments like this, when

I glance backward and feel the tide of life and memory rushing forward, I am torn between gratitude for what was given and longing for what was lost.

Dancing through the night last night, my heart was full of joy. Randy and I were joined by a delicious assortment of men of all varieties. There was Paul, who as the minister of one of the largest Unity Churches in America is fundamentally changing the way that denomination—as well as many others—accept and embrace gay men. At one point in the evening, we encountered a handsome man who described himself to me as a writer, and despite my misinterpretation of Randy's raised eyebrows, I sipped my drink and casually asked what he had written, only to discover to my embarrassment that the man who stood before me was one of my most revered writers. His novel *The Hours* has never ceased to inspire me to dig deeper as a writer, and maybe one day, I might write something so truly touching, raw, and authentic. It was a night of bliss that ended with all of us sitting on the curb, eating pizza and basking in the warm ocean breeze that caresses the streets and whisks away the cares of all those who travel those centuries-old cobbled paths, which were initially tread by the Pilgrims on their voyage to freedom and acceptance.

It is here, in this dialectical paradox, suspended between joy and tragedy, freedom and shame-induced bondage, great talent and squandered existence, that *The Velvet Rage* lives. As gay men, we have been anything but ordinary and predictable. Everywhere you turn, and no matter what age, station in life, and economic status, the lives of gay men of all shapes and sizes contain this polar mix of pain and ecstasy. Our problems and successes in life are truly no different than any other man's, and yet we are uniquely identifiable in our ways—there is no mistaking gay culture when you see it. We are in no way more pathological or deviant than any other man who has walked this planet, present or past. And yet, we are clearly different. When you love a man, it fundamentally changes you—and we have all been shaped by our love of men; the heavy caress of his hand, the brush of the hair on his forearm, and the powerful kiss that at once dominates and deconstructs our defenses. These things enliven our days and fuel our dreams.

In the years since *The Velvet Rage* was originally published, so many men have been generous with me and shared their stories and struggle with shame. It is the concept of shame, in fact, that has enlightened so many of their lives. Prior to reading the book, they felt they had long ago been done with the ravages of shame over their sexual orientation. Some actually have no memory of feeling shame over being gay—they marched out of the closet at a young age and never looked back. It is here, at this point, that a truly life-changing insight emerges. Most of us have not felt the emotion of shame for many years—since we first came to terms with being gay. For the majority of gay men who are out of the closet, shame is no longer *felt*. What was once a feeling has become something deeper and more sinister in our psyches—it is a deeply and rigidly held belief in our own unworthiness for love. We were taught by the experience of shame during those tender and formative years of adolescence that there was something about us that was flawed, in essence unlovable, and that we must go about the business of making ourselves lovable if we are to survive. We were hungry for love, and our very existence depended upon it, as the British psychiatrist R. D. Laing noted: "Whether life is worth living depends on whether there is love in life." The lesson of that early, crippling shame was imprinted on our lives. *If you are to be loved, you must hide the truth about yourself and work at being lovable.*

The days of feeling shame over being gay passed by us like the last days of summer, slipping into our memory as we moved on with life and went about the business of openly living as gay men. Shame became embedded into the trunk of our ever-expanding personalities, affecting everything about us, and yet so minutely close to the core of our being that we are helpless to see it as different than "me." As the eye cannot see itself, we cannot see or feel this embedded shame. But make no mistake, the shame is there—and it is very real.

Of all the comments readers have shared with me over these past six years, the one that comes up most often is: "I don't *feel* shame." Very few of us feel the shame, but almost all of us struggle with the private belief that "if you really knew the whole, un-varnished truth about me, you would know that I am unlovable." It is this belief that pushes us, even dominates us with its tyranny of existential angst. In our own way, young and old alike, we set about the business of "earning" love, and escaping the pain of believing we are unlovable. It is this damned quest that pushes us to the highest of highs, and simultaneously brings us to the brink. This is both the creator of the fabulous gay man and his destroyer.

Shame is not the same thing as homophobia. Homophobia is the fear of being gay, and shame is the fear of being unlovable. You can relatively easily cure the homophobia, but the shame, without vigilant care and attention, will last a lifetime. Gay shame is not embarrassment over being gay; it is the belief that being gay is a mere symptom of your own mortally flawed psyche. You can treat the homophobic symptom, but the underlying disease persists until acknowledged and treated.

From this perspective, I have come to understand why *The Velvet Rage* continues to touch so many younger gay men, many of whom never experienced the protracted coming-out process that others of us lived through during a time when there was far less social acceptance of being gay. Even though they may not have experienced embarrassment over being gay, they grew up with the knowledge that they were different from their parents (who are typically straight) and much of the world around them. Knowing they were different in such a significant way led them to internalize the beliefs of shame. The statistics continue to bear out that gay men in their early twenties are increasingly likely to struggle with addiction, depression, and even suicide—all symptoms of the man who bears the pain of feeling unlovable.

Some have asked, if the world becomes more accepting of being gay, won't that lessen the relevance of shame in gay men? Ideally, yes, it will. However, what is equally true is that as homophobia diminishes in society, it is not a given that gay men will no longer experience the isolation that comes from feeling different than one's peers and family. It is in this experience of differentness, being the one who doesn't fit in, that shame takes root in our lives. So it follows that even as homophobia begins to wane in our world, gay men will still need to do the work of acknowledging all the ways in which we have accepted our unlovableness and actively do the work required to obliterate such heinous beliefs from our lives. In the decade and a half since Ellen DeGeneres came out as a lesbian on national television and the openly gay sitcom *Will and Grace* first aired, much has changed throughout the world regarding the acceptability of being gay. During this same period of time, addiction and mental health issues among gay men have continued at alarmingly high levels, and all indications are that they continue to rise. While social acceptance of gay men, gay rights, and gay marriage is critically important to the well-being of gay men, these things are not sufficient to inspire us to do the deeper work of healing the tight grip of shame on our lives.

This revised edition of *The Velvet Rage* contains an expanded final chapter with practical information on how to live an authentic life as a gay man without the influence of shame. It is a struggle to live authentically, without the need to compensate for our inadequacies or to escape the pain of our emotions through addictions. Much of what I write throughout the book is influenced by my own training in Dialectical Behavior Therapy (DBT), and I owe an enormous debt of gratitude to psychologist, researcher, and Zen practitioner Marsha Linehan, who created DBT. DBT was recently listed in a *Time* magazine supplement on "100 New Scientific Discoveries." For those who might be interested in doing further psychotherapy on the issues of shame and emotion regulation, I recommend that you find a therapist who practices DBT. While not all DBT therapists are familiar with the issues specific to gay men, I find them to be generally well-trained and highly consistent with the approach taken in *The Velvet Rage*.

As this summer fades into autumn, and I leave the windswept dunes of Cape Cod and return to my practice in Los Angeles, I reflect back on the thousands of letters and e-mails I've received from readers of *The Velvet Rage*. Most gay men and their families found the book to be helpful, and a few have been enraged by it; but it is difficult, if not impossible, to be neutral about the gay shame of which I write. The book has reached far beyond what I ever dreamed possible, touching the lives of tens of thousands of gay men around the world. It is my sincere hope that this revised edition will continue that tradition and breathe life into a message that I believe is desperately needed among gay men.

No other group of people on this planet is better equipped to bring the message of self-acceptance and authenticity to the world than gay men and women. Many of us have struggled mightily with shame and learning to access the power of authenticity and honesty that lies within us. Whether it was the killing of eight million Jews; the bombing of the Federal Building in Oklahoma City that took 168 lives, including nineteen children; or the heinous act of hijacking and flying commercial aircraft into heavily populated high-rise buildings, the lives of nearly all destructive perpetrators are intertwined with, and in many cases motivated by, rageful reactions to personal shame. The devastating effects of shame are ubiquitous, and the message of self-acceptance is universally craved by a world that has in large part been taught that you aren't young, thin, holy, rich, or successful enough. It has taken me nearly fifty years to understand the enormous importance of overcoming destructive shame in healing our lives, and even in healing an entire planet that seems to be flirting all too closely with calamity.

As gay men, we are uniquely qualified to bring the message of compassion, forgiveness, and self-acceptance—for we have been there and know how important it is to be proud of who we are. The destructive influences of shame are everywhere in our world, and it is my sincere hope that this book will start a movement that takes us beyond this current age of gay self-indulgence and overcompensation and instead pushes us on the world stage as the leaders of self-acceptance and awareness. Although some may see this as too grandiose a vision, I do not. It is the natural outcome of our own struggle with shame that we would share our insight with a planet that desperately needs it. In this spirit, it is my dream *The Velvet Rage* will bring a deep change within you and every reader who picks it up, and together we start a movement that frees our world from all the ways in which shame blocks people everywhere from experiencing the joy and contentment that lays just beyond those dark walls that imprison the human spirit.

Because this hard-won message of self-acceptance is so critically important, not only to gay men but to all, I offer this revised edition. While virtually all of the original material from the book remains both in this text and, more importantly, in practical relevance, I have added new material that I believe is essential. Chapter 14, which describes the skills important to overcoming shame and living an authentic life, has been revised and significantly expanded. While understanding the origins of shame-based wounds is important, this alone is not sufficient to bring needed change into our lives. Change comes by choice and practice, not from insight about our past. This is, I feel, the most important chapter in the book.

This edition closes with a newly added epilogue about my life and my own struggle with shame. I thought long and hard before including this, as the telling of one's own story always seems to have a tinge of self-absorption and even grandiosity, but two reasons pushed me to include this brief memoir of my adult life. First, I find that I often learn best through stories that help me to develop a mental picture of a complex issue. *The Velvet Rage* is filled with stories from the lives of my patients, so I thought it only appropriate to offer my own story, for whatever value the reader might find in it. Second, and of great importance to me personally, I discuss my experience of being HIV-positive for almost a quarter of a century. I have held great shame about being HIV-positive, and for the first time in these pages, I share with you as honestly as I am capable my experience of living with HIV. For so many gay men, the shame over being HIV-positive runs a deeper and more destructive course than the shame over being gay. It becomes something of a lifelong reminder that we are flawed and enlivens the deeply held, sinister belief that perhaps HIV is physical evidence of our own unloveableness. In the telling of my story, I hope to reach out to all—straight, gay, HIV-positive, and -negative—to offer compassion, acceptance, and, most of all, the hope that comes from knowing that no matter who you are or what you have done, you are worthy of love.

Alan Downs
Los Angeles, California
August 2011

INTRODUCTION

The experience of being a gay man in the twenty-first century is different from that of any other minority, sexual orientation, gender, or culture grouping. We are different from, on the one hand, women, and on the other hand, straight men. Our lives are a unique blending of testosterone and gentleness, hypersexuality and delicate sensuality, rugged masculinity and refined gentility. There is no other group quite like that of gay men. We are a culture of our own.

It is upon this important and undeniable cornerstone that this book was written. Understanding our differences, loving ourselves without judgment, and at the same time noticing what makes us fulfilled, empowered, and loving men are the forces that converged in the conceiving, planning, writing, and publishing of this book.

While we are different, we are at the same time very similar to all others. We want to be loved and to love. We want to find some joy in life. We hope to fall asleep at night fulfilled from our day's endeavors. In these aspirations and appetites we are like all men and women. The problem is, our path to fulfilling these basic human needs has proven to be fundamentally different from the well-worn paths of straight humanity.

Some have said that we must blaze our own trail and not be lured into the ways of the straight man. We must be brave enough to honor rather than hide our differences. We must stand up and fight for the right to be gay and all that it means.

In this book, you will find an honest and more complete picture of what it is to be a gay man in today's world. Yes, we have more sexual partners in a lifetime than any other grouping of people. And at the same time, we also have among the highest rates of depression and suicide, not to mention sexually transmitted diseases. As a group we tend to be more emotionally expressive than other men, and yet our relationships are far shorter on average than those of straight men. We have more expendable income, more expensive houses, and more fashionable cars, clothes, and furniture than just about any other cultural group. But are we truly happier?

The disturbing truth is that we aren't any happier, by virtually any index measured today. Much the opposite is true. Psychotherapy offices the world over are frequented by gay men struggling to find some joy and fulfillment in life. Substance abuse clinics across the country—from The Betty Ford Center in California to The Menninger Clinic in Texas to Beth Israel Medical Center in New York City—are filled with far more gay men than would be indicated by our proportions in the general population. It's safe to estimate that virtually every gay man has wondered on more than a few occasions if it is truly possible to be consistently happy and a gay man.

When you look around it becomes somewhat undeniable that we are a wounded lot. Somehow, the life we are living isn't leading us to a better, more fulfilled psychological and emotional place. Instead, we seem to struggle more, suffer more, and want more. The gay life isn't cutting it for most of us.

Some ill-informed, closed-minded people would say that it is our sexual appetite for man-on-man sex that has made lasting happiness illusive. If we would just be "normal," find a good woman and settle down, then we'd discover what life is all about.

That's just crazy. Our struggles have nothing to do with loving men per se. Substance abuse, hypersexuality, short-lived relationships, depression, sexually transmitted diseases, the insatiable hunger for more and better, and the need to decorate our worlds to cover up seamy truths—these are our torments. Becoming a fulfilled gay man is not about trying to become "not gay," but has everything to do with finding a way through this world that affords us our share of joy, happiness, fulfillment, and love.

In my practice as a psychologist, this is my goal: to help gay men be gay *and* fulfilled. The lessons I've learned from the profound teachers in my life—my gay male patients—are collected in this book. Their struggles, disappointments, and ultimate achievements are chronicled here. While names, identities, and geographic locations have all been changed to protect their rightful anonymity, I have made every possible attempt to be faithful to the relevant facts.

The book is arranged into a simple three-stage model that describes the journey of virtually all gay men with whom I have worked. I suspect that this model, or some modified version of it, is likely to be universal to all gay men in the western world and perhaps across the globe.

The stages are arranged by the primary manner in which the gay man handles shame. The first stage is "Overwhelmed by Shame" and includes that period of time when he remained "in the closet" and fearful of his own sexuality. The second stage is "Compensating for Shame" and describes the gay man's attempt to neutralize his shame by being more successful, outrageous, fabulous, beautiful, or masculine. During this stage he may take on many sexual partners in his attempt to make himself feel attractive, sexy, and loved—in short, less shameful.

The final stage is "Cultivating Authenticity." Not all gay men progress out of the previous two stages, but those who do begin to build a life that is based upon their own passions and values rather than proving to themselves that they are desirable and lovable.

The goal of this book is to help gay men achieve this third stage of authenticity. It is my experience that gay men who are not ready or willing to work toward this goal have a difficult time acknowledging their shame and the radical effects of it on their lives. Until a gay man is ready to reexamine his life, he may not be able to realize the undercurrent of shame that has carried him into a life that often isn't very fulfilling.

My own trek from shame to authenticity as a gay man has mirrored that of many of my clients' stories that I share with you throughout the book. Having grown up in a Christian fundamentalist home in Louisiana, I entered my adult years struggling with my own sexuality. After being married for several years and spending even more years in therapy, I began to accept myself for the man that I am, not the one that I or my family had wished for.

When I came out of the closet, I stepped right into the middle of the gay explosion in San Francisco during the 1980s. It was an exciting and horrible time—there were more men than I'd ever seen before and so many of them were dying from AIDS. Since then, I've lived in some of the gayest cities in the country: New York City, New Orleans, Key West, and Fort Lauderdale. There's not much that I haven't seen and tried.

Early in my career, I abandoned clinical psychology to become an executive at Hewlett Packard. It was the go-go '80s, and everyone, including me, was hoping to strike it rich in Silicone Valley. Part of my own journey toward authenticity forced me to confront my career choices and return to my real passion: clinical psychology. So I did, and it turned out to be one of the best decisions of my life. My life and my work have taken on a depth of meaning and fulfillment that I would have never known otherwise. I spend my days, among other things, helping gay men to heal the wounds of being gay in a straight world, and in so doing, realize their own authenticity and fulfillment. They have been my teachers and mentors, reminding me daily of the importance of staying true to myself regardless of how others may view me. It is their stories, not mine, that fill these pages. What wisdom is contained between these covers is theirs, and anything less is more than likely my doing.

It must be noted that what is written here is in many ways applicable to lesbian women, too. While I do work with many lesbian women and find their journey to be similar, the ways in which it is explored are often very different. For example, lesbian women aren't known to frequent bathhouses, sex clubs, or driven to decorate their lives like gay men. They express their struggle with shame differently and in a uniquely female way. So it is out of respect for lesbian women that this book is written about gay men only. To be more inclusive of the lesbian experience would undoubtedly result in a book that does the lesbian experience an injustice. The stages of their lives are the same; however, the way in which they unfold is often very different.

Finally, a word about the differences between straight and gay men should be included. Often people will ask me, "Isn't the struggle with shame similar for straight men?" To this, I would also answer yes, but not in the same way. Straight men struggle with their own authenticity and intimate relationships. And yes, they do struggle with shame that is created by a culture that has taught them to hold a masculine ideal that is unachievable, if not downright cruel. But as with lesbian women—and to a far greater degree—their struggles look very different. For example, straight men may fight shame by always having a cute, young, blonde bombshell of a woman on their arm (as some gay men do with a cute, young, blond bombshell of a man), but the constraints of living in a straight culture and mores cause their experience to be quite different than that of gay men. One should not conclude from these pages that straight men are even one fraction healthier than gay men. What is being said is that the trauma of growing up gay in a world that is run primarily by straight men is deeply wounding in a unique and profound way. Straight men have other issues and struggles that are no less wounding but are quite different from those of gay men.

I have written this book as a heart-to-heart talk with gay men that I invite you, the straight reader, to participate in. It seemed the most compassionate and useful voice given the difficulty of the material I present. After all, much of what I write about is the darker, more unseemly side of gay life to which our straight friends and family are not often exposed and, truth be told, which we'd rather that they didn't know about. So I have written it as a gay man who has experienced all of this and more, writing to an audience of gay men who know of what I speak. To adopt a more clinical, third person voice would, in many ways, bring an unnecessary coldness to an otherwise close and intimate exploration of our lives.

THE ROOTS OF RAGE

"The truth is rarely pure and never simple."

OSCAR WILDE
The Importance of Being Earnest

Chapter 1

THE LITTLE BOY WITH
THE BIG SECRET

We are all born into this world helpless, love-starved creatures. For the first years of life, we are completely dependent upon others for everything we need, both physically and emotionally. As we grow to be children, the world still doesn't make complete sense to us; we still need someone to take care of us.

This craving for love and protection is more than just a passing urge or momentary appetite. It is an irrepressible drive and a constant longing that, when unfulfilled, will last a good long time, likely into adulthood.

For the early years of life, the only source that could satisfy your enormous cravings and needs was your parents. They provided you with everything you needed, but couldn't satisfy for yourself. Long before you reached the age of verbal thought, you knew that you needed your parents. You knew their touch and smell. You anticipated their caresses and recoiled at their scolding.

At that early age, abandonment by your parents was akin to death, and you avoided abandonment at all costs. In your own childish ways, you did everything within your power to retain the attention and love of your parents. Even when you screamed and threw tantrums, you were not risking their ire so much as desperately trying to keep your parents from ignoring you.

But perhaps starting at the ages of four to six, your parents realized that you were different. They didn't know exactly how or why, but you were definitely not quite like the other children they had known. It may have had little or no influence on their love for you, but they may have treated you in a different manner than your siblings or differently than your friends' parents treated them.

You, too, began to understand that you were different. Your understanding was only dim at first, but as those early years progressed into adolescence, you became increasingly aware that you weren't like other boys—maybe even not like your parents.

Along with the growing knowledge that we were different was an equally expanding fear that our "different-ness" would cause us to lose the love and affection of our parents. This terror of

> "I did the usual stuff in school . . . played sports and dated girls in junior high and high school. No matter what I did, though, I always had this feeling that I was different. It's funny, whenever one of my buddies would steal his father's *Playboy*, we'd take it out into the field behind the 7–11 to look at the pictures and smoke cigarettes. I remember being more interested in how my buddies were reacting to the pictures of naked women than in the actual pictures, and I also remember fantasizing about what kind of a man gets to have women like these. All my buddies wanted to do is talk about the big tits of the women, so I'd go along with it just for show."
>
> KAL FROM OMAHA, NE

being abandoned, alone, and unable to survive forced us to find a way—*any way*—to retain our parents' love. We couldn't change ourselves, but we could change the way we acted. We could hide our differences, ingratiate ourselves to our mothers, and distance ourselves from our fathers whom we somehow knew would destroy us if he discovered our true nature.

And we didn't hide our true selves just from our parents. As best we could, we hid the truth from everyone, especially from other children. Children, probably more than any other people, are keenly aware of differences in one another, and often torment other children they perceive as different. Indeed, if you want to see some of the cruelest human behavior, just watch a kindergarten playground for a while. Children are merciless—especially when they sense that another child is different.

Maybe you remember just how cruel children can be? Most gay men have early memories of this kind of rejection at the hands of their playmates. In fact, it is on the playground that we probably first began to consciously think about how we were different from other boys. We didn't necessarily want to play the same games as the other boys. We were taunted or ignored by the more athletic, aggressive boys who always seemed to win the positive attention of their classmates and even the teachers. Maybe you also taunted and teased in a futile attempt to fit in.

> "I can't remember when it started, but I can definitely remember always feeling like I didn't fit in. I can remember sitting alone on the playground even when I was in kindergarten. I didn't want to do all the stupid things the other boys were doing like sword fighting with sticks or playing cowboys and Indians. Even back then it all seemed so strange to me."
>
> DALE FROM CHARLESTON, NC

It was this early abuse suffered at the hands of our peers, coupled with the fear of rejection by our parents, that engrained in us one very strident lesson: *There was something about us that was disgusting, aberrant, and essentially unlovable.*

We decided whatever it was—at the time we still may not have known what it was—must be hidden completely from view. Although we are older now, we are still driven by those insatiable, infantile drives for love and acceptance. In order to survive, we learned to become something that we thought would be more acceptable to our parents, teachers, and playmates.

> "I hated school. I always made sure I arrived just before the morning bell and went straight home after school. I especially hated physical education. It never failed that when the teams were picked, I was always the last one. None of the boys wanted me on their team. They'd laugh and call me 'sissy' . . . "
>
> TOM FROM PORTLAND, OR

We made ourselves more acceptable to others in a variety of ways. Perhaps you learned that you could win approval by becoming more sensitive than the other boys. Maybe you learned that you could win approval by displaying a creativity that the other boys refused to show, or you learned to win approval by excelling at everything you did. You may have even tried to earn affection by withdrawing and becoming helpless, hoping to arouse the sympathies of others.

The essence of all these experiences was the same. No matter how we expressed it, we needed love *and we feared that there was something about us that made us unlovable.* It was an experience that became an integral part of our psychology that has stayed with us most of our lives. We became utterly convinced that there was something about us that is essentially unlovable.

THE FIRST MAN IN
YOUR LIFE

So where were our fathers when this was happening? Why didn't they rise to our rescue and teach us that being a man starts by being honest about yourself? Why couldn't they see our dilemma, the fear in our eyes, take us by the hand, and teach us how to calm the angst and love ourselves?

In the book *Silent Sons*, Robert Ackerman gives us a clue to the emotional absence of our fathers:

He is like no other man in the world. His influence is legendary. Without his so much as moving a finger, his look can give approval or stop you dead in your tracks. Without his saying a word, his silence says it all. He is a man who can seem capable of all feats in the world; a man who appears immortal and is supposed to live forever, or at least never grow old. He is a man of great emotions—if you could figure them out. A man of many contradictions and secrets. A man who wants to be close, but teaches independence. A man who stops hugging boys once they become 12. A man who has anger but won't tolerate it in others. A man whose physical body eventually declines, but whose emotional influence continues to grow even after he is gone.[1]

> "I honestly don't think I was one bit smarter than any of the other kids in my grade. I just figured out that if I studied hard and read everything I could, my teachers seemed to like me more. By the time I got to junior high, I discovered a small group of other good students to hang out with. For the first time, I remember feeling like I belonged somewhere."
>
> RICK FROM SAN FRANCISCO, CA

As a young gay man, the first man you loved was your father, and you craved from him love, affection, and tenderness. What most of us received from our fathers fell far short. Why? To start with, our fathers were raised, as we were, to be tough, stable, and emotionally detached. On top of that, many of them were veterans of wars that forced them at a young age to suppress their emotions and to commit unspeakable acts against humanity in the name of patriotism. In sum, many of our fathers grew up in a culture that offered them power in exchange for stoicism and buried emotion. As we grew older, we acted differently than the straight boys did. Those boys often pushed us aside, as different and strange, as did many of our fathers, too. Perhaps they were threatened by their own homoerotic fantasies, or maybe they just didn't know how to handle us and so they retreated in confusion. Whatever the cause, most of us grew into our young adulthoods without having had a truly loving, honest, and safe relationship with a man. Not with our buddies, and certainly not with our fathers. The natural and organic expectation of a boy is that he will be nurtured and cared for by both a mother *and* a father. It was an agreement that was written into the genetic code of our souls—our fathers would love and lead us, and in exchange we would respect and honor them. For many of us, our fathers broke this agreement at a very tender time in our lives.

> "I never spoke with my father about my being gay. Years ago I told my mother and, of course, I knew she'd tell my dad. I know that he knew, but we never talked about it. I just couldn't bear to see the disappointment in his face. Now that he's gone, I grieve for him—and for us—when I think about it, because we never were able to be friends. Friends? Hell, we weren't even able to talk."
>
> TOM FROM SEATTLE, WA

Of all the invalidation we will receive in our lives, this is by far the most damaging. The first man that we love—arguably the man we will love the most in our life—is incapable of validating us at a time when we need it most. It is emotional betrayal of the worst sort. The wound created by this betrayal will go on to affect us throughout most of our lives.

Our mother, too, likely sensed that we were different. She moved in to protect us from what she rightly sensed would be a slow and subtle betrayal by our fathers. She nurtured. She favored us. She over-validated us to compensate for the betrayal she saw us suffer.

The end result of these strained family dynamics was that the only authentic validation we may have experienced as a young man came from our mothers. And this validation was usually directed at the things that our mothers valued—the feminine ideals. Hence, the feminine qualities (not to be confused with *effeminate* qualities) of our true self were validated the most.

Psychologically speaking, this made us comfortable, even drawn to the feminine, and resulted in a better-developed tender side. We cultivated creative, compassionate, and nurturing talents. In addition, we became comfortable in the company of women. While this wasn't true for all of us—some of us had fathers who were emotionally present regardless of our sexuality— it was true for many of us, to a greater or lesser extent.

So as mere children, years before we would have sex for the first time with a man, we had suffered rejection by our peers, emotional neglect from our fathers, and overcompensating protection from our mothers. We survived by learning to conform to the expectations of others at a time in our development when we should have been learning to follow our own internal promptings. We became puppets of a sort—allowing those around us to pull the strings that made us act in acceptable ways, all the while knowing that we couldn't trust ourselves.

What would you like me to be? A great student? A priest in the church? Mother's little man? The first-chair violinist? We became dependent on adopting the skin our environment imposed upon us to earn the love and affection we craved. How could we love ourselves when everything around us told us that we were unlovable? Instead, we chased the affection, approval, and attention doled out by others.

Not surprisingly, the long-term effect was an inability to validate ourselves. The ability to derive internal satisfaction and contentment didn't emerge from our adolescence as it should have. Instead, we sputtered along looking to others for the confidence and well-being that we needed to protect ourselves from being overcome with shame. What normally becomes an internal, self-sustaining process of self-validation in the healthy, young adult remained infantile within us, and we instead became sophisticated in the ways of coercing acceptance from the world around us.

So the little boy with the big secret becomes the man who is driven to avoid shame by hiding his dark truth. Famished for authentic validation and without a reliable sense of self-direction, he develops a sophisticated radar for those things and people who will make him feel good about himself.

This little boy grows up to be a man who is supremely knowledgeable of culture and fashion. A man of Adonis-sized proportions and many lovers. A man of great success and wealth. A fabulous and outrageous host. An arbiter of good taste and elegant design. A pop-culture aficionado.

To a great extent, these are the gay men we have known. This is you and me—a little boy with a terrible secret who hides his curse behind a curtain made of crimson velvet. It may surprise many to learn that his secret is not his sexual appetite for men. No, it is something darker, stinging, and filled with rage.

His secret he cannot reveal, not even to himself, for fear that it will consume him completely. Deep inside, far from the light of awareness, the secret lives. Go down beneath the layers of public façade, personal myth, and fantasy. Peel away the well-crafted layers, for only then can you see the secret clearly for what it is: his own self-hatred.

Chapter 2

UGLY TRUTHS &
HIGH-FASHION DREAMS

"I guess my worst fear is that I will become a bitter, lonely old queen hanging on to a bar stool in some dark joint where nobody goes. I mean it isn't getting old that worries me—it's being old and alone that terrifies me. I look around and I don't see one of my friends in a happy relationship. We're all pretty much in the same boat. We date. We fall in love. We fall out of love or get dumped. We are single again. After a while, we've all sort of given up on finding Mr. Right. It's more about are you Mr. In-My-Bed-Right-Now and, whatever you do, please don't stay for breakfast. If you do, we'll eventually end up hating each other."

JOHN FROM SAN FRANCISCO, CA

In modern history, there's never been an easier time to be gay. Sure, we've got a few crazed, right-wing enemies, but it's only a matter of time before their homophobic finger-wagging is considered a mistake in the service of social evolution—like the McCarthy-era speeches and racially motivated lynchings. There is a real sense that social attitudes and values toward gay men are shifting for the better. Times are definitely changing.

Yet in my work as a psychologist, my clients who are gay men sometimes talk about being despondent, depressed, even suicidal. They tell me about the constant struggle to find fulfillment and lasting love. Some recount stories about lots of sex, with lots of different men at exotic parties in the finest locations around the globe. Others confess feeling over-the-hill at thirty-five, as if life were over because the twenty-somethings no longer want them. Still others are caught up in their own world of money, art, fashion, and palatial homes.

Virtually all of the gay men I work with agree on one thing: no matter how accepting society becomes, it is still very hard to be a gay man *and* a truly happy person. We may have gained so much, but something critical is still missing.

If you're "out," you no longer harbor that "dirty little secret" about yourself, but you likely do continue to hide your true self behind the beauty you manufacture. And nobody knows how to create style more than gay men. We decorate the world. We decorate our lives. We decorate our bodies. And we do it all in an effort to hide our real selves from the world. Gay men are the worldwide experts on style, fashion, etiquette, bodybuilding, art, and design. In every one of these fields gay men predominate. If this weren't so, there would be few tuning in to the hit television show *Queer Eye for the Straight Guy*.

We specialize in makeovers of all types and sizes. We're experts in making things and people *look good*. We are professionals in remodeling ugly truths into high-fashion dreams.

Ever stop to wonder why this is so? Is there really a gay creativity gene that we all inherited? When you think about it, is it actually plausible that our sexual orientation genetics would somehow also give us a talent for hair, makeup, and rearranging the living room?

I don't think so. There seems to be something more to it. Something about the experience of being gay causes us to develop our "fashion" skills. Something about growing up gay forced us to learn how to hide ugly realities behind a finely crafted façade.

Why is this so? We hid because we learned that hiding is a means to survival. The naked truth about who we are wasn't acceptable, so we learned to hide behind a beautiful image. We learned to split ourselves in parts, hiding what wasn't acceptable and flaunting what was. We learned to wave beautiful, colorful scarves to distract attention from our gayness—like the matador waving a red scarf before the bull to distract the beast from goring his body. We became experts in crafting outrageous scarves.

The truth is that we grew up disabled. Not disabled by our homosexuality, but emotionally disabled by an environment that taught us we were unacceptable, not "real" men and therefore, shameful. As young boys, we too readily internalized those strong feelings of shame into a core belief: *I am unacceptably flawed.* It crippled our sense of self and prevented us from following the normal, healthy stages of adolescent development. We were consumed with the task of hiding the fundamental truth of ourselves from the world around us and pretending to be something we weren't. At the time, it seemed the only way to survive.

One cannot be around gay men without noticing that we are a wonderful and wounded lot. Beneath our complex layers lies a deeper secret that covertly corrodes our lives. The seeds of this secret were not planted by us, but by a world that didn't understand us, wanted to change us, and at times, was fiercely hostile to us.

It's not about how good or bad we are. It's about the struggle so many of us have experienced growing up gay in a world that didn't accept us, and the ongoing struggle as adult gay men to create lives that are happy, fulfilling, and ultimately free of shame.

This life we created for ourselves—the one that we thought gay men were supposed to be enjoying—can be empty and unfulfilling. But we're stuck in a role—a way of life—that is rooted in our shame and holds us back from creating the life we really want. Somewhere along the way, we picked up the idea that a happy gay man was one who had lots of sex and at least one handsome man on his arm at all times. Wherever this "ideal" of gay men is featured, such as in entertainment or advertising, they are depicted as handsome, muscular men who seem to have it all—sensitivity, stylish good looks, and a body that would drive Cleopatra *and* Marc Anthony wild with desire.

> "The nurse asked me at the clinic how many sexual partners I'd had in the past year. It took me by surprise—do I tell the truth or lie? I told him about half a dozen, which is an out-and-out lie. I have no idea. The truth is, I really don't want to think about it. I'm sure it's somewhere in the dozens, if not more. . . "
>
> KIRBY FROM DALLAS, TX

Virtually all of gay culture is defined by sex and the pursuit of desire and beauty. Whether it's a gay bar or a gay news magazine, the hard-driving, heart-pounding message of sex is omnipresent. And it's not just sex—it's toe-curling, mind-blowing, hard-body, all-night-long sex.

Is this enough? I am a man. I need to be loved. I need to love myself. I need to feel strong *and* to cry. I need to feel alive *and* to grieve my losses. I need to know that there is someone in this world who truly loves me. I need to love someone. I need a safe, stable, and committed home. Truth is, I need all these things much more than I need great sex.

Even though we never talk about such things at the cocktail parties and catered affairs we attend, we crave it with a desire that we can barely conceal. Behind the façade, we are honestly and without reservation human. And it's past time for us to realize that living the ideal gay life isn't humane in the least.

Remember when you first knew you were gay and imagined how your life would be? You probably imagined meeting a handsome fellow, falling madly in love, and living your lives together with a few dogs or, if you were really progressive, even children. You imagined your family would eventually accept your lover as a part of the family and you'd live happily together for a lifetime.

> "I never imagined that I would be single again at forty. This isn't at all how I thought my life would turn out. I wasn't like the others. . . I thought I'd find a good, stable lover and we'd be together forever. Now I'm not sure whether to crawl under a rock, get a face-lift, or take up bowling. I mean, how do you meet a nice guy?
>
> TOM FROM VANCOUVER, BC

Okay, maybe that was just my fantasy. But I'll bet anything that yours was equally rosy. Then, somewhere along the way, your dream died. A lover betrayed you. You couldn't be faithful to one man. Boyfriend after boyfriend proved to be untrustworthy. The men you desired and loved disappointed you.

What did you do? You went to the gym, to the bathhouse, to the bars, to the sex club, or maybe even tried to lose yourself in climbing the corporate ladder. You tried to convince yourself that you weren't unhappy, just bored. Or maybe you just weren't getting enough sex. Or maybe this time, after test-driving dozens of models, you'd find the right man for you. Who knows, maybe

Quentin Crisp's "tall, dark man" was just around the corner—or maybe just in the next bed?

But as dear Mr. Crisp reports, the tall, dark man never comes. What to do? Bury the sadness deep within yourself and keep moving lest you find yourself suffocating in your own self-pity.

Why are my intimate relationships short-lived? Why am I so driven to have the perfect body, the most beautiful house, the most fabulous career, the youngest and prettiest boyfriend, etc.? Why do I fight this nagging depression that tells me my life is bereft of greater meaning?

What all of these questions point to is an emotional wound. It is a wound that almost all gay men experience, and if they choose to move their lives forward, must also heal. If you're asking these questions, as have I and most of the gay men I encounter, you're struggling with this wound inside yourself, too.

The wound is the trauma caused by exposure to overwhelming shame at an age when you weren't equipped to cope with it. An emotional wound caused by toxic shame is a very serious and persistent disability that has the potential to literally destroy your life. It is much more than just a poor self-image. It is the internalized and deeply held belief that you are somehow unacceptable, unlovable, shameful, and in short, flawed.

What makes the wound of shame so destructive? To experience such shame, particularly during our childhood and adolescent years, prevents us from developing a strong sense of self.

A sense of self is the development of a strong identity that is validated by your environment. The nerdy teenager develops an identity that includes "science genius" because among other things, he joined the science or math club and discovered other teenagers who validated his talent. Same thing for the jocks and head-bangers—they developed a sense of self from the validation they received by hanging out with others who share and value similar interests and abilities.

Straight boys developed their sense of their sexual self by taking girls out on dates. Everyone, including their parents, validated them for this behavior. Hence, they came to accept it as part of themselves. Gay men, on the other hand, rarely had this experience. In large part, we played the part and took girls to the prom so that we'd fit in, all the while knowing it was a farce. Although we received validation for our actions, it was meaningless because we knew at the deepest level that we were play-acting. Consequently, we developed a pseudo-self, which wasn't a natural growth of our abilities, desires, and intelligence. It was a self that would earn us validation by others, but our true selves remained hidden from everyone.

Our core belief that one is unacceptably flawed prevented our organic self from developing as it does in an emotionally healthy boy. Instead, it became frozen in time, undeveloped, and somewhat juvenile in form. How we coped was by presenting to the world a self that was explicitly designed to help us get by.

We all seek validation every day. It is one of the essential psychological needs of every person.

For example, when you are at work and make a comment during a meeting, you want to know that you were heard by those present. They don't have to agree with you (although agreement would be perceived as even more validating), just hear what you had to say. To take this example a step further, imagine speaking up at a meeting and in the middle of your comment, someone else starts talking. That would be experienced as invalidating, and you would probably attempt to make your comment again.

When you come home from work that night, you tell your partner about your day. If he ignores you, falls asleep while you're talking, or immediately starts talking about his day, you'll likely feel further dismissed and invalidated. What you want from your partner at that moment is recognition that you may have had a difficult day at work.

When you really pay attention, you realize that much of life's everyday pleasure and frustration comes from either being validated or invalidated, even in interactions with complete strangers. You complain at the restaurant about your meal, and the waiter whisks it away for improvement. That's validating. If he were to argue with you and tell you that the meal is perfectly fine the way it is, that's invalidating.

As you have probably noticed, there are different levels of validation. Just being acknowledged, recognized, or heard is a low-level form of validation. Having someone genuinely compliment you is a higher level of validation. In most everyday situations, we are seeking low-level validation. We don't need complete agreement or compliments (although these are awfully nice to receive), just acknowledgement and a little understanding will do.

The only type of validation that really counts, however, is authentic validation. For example, if you go to see your therapist and he responds to everything you say with standard phrases like "Tell me more . . ." or "That's interesting . . ." while not offering concrete advice or analysis, his interest in you begins to feel false and, consequently, less validating. Or, for example, if you drive your neighbor's new convertible to the store and get lots of compliments on it, you're not likely to feel all that validated since it really isn't your car. Authentic validation is honest validation of something that matters to you.

Why is *authentic* validation important? Because when we are validated for a pretense, the validation is hollow, it's baseless, it's not at all satisfying. For example, if you had someone else write your term paper for a class and you subsequently received an "A" on it, that isn't validating. Or more to the point, when a gay man presents a false, inauthentic self to the world and is subsequently validated for that façade, he will feel hollow, and the validation won't be satisfying.

The young gay boy who learns to "fake out" everyone and act straight becomes starved for authentic validation. He immediately and unconsciously discounts all validation since he knows what he is presenting to others isn't authentic.

Authentic validation is absolutely necessary for the development of a strong sense of self. Without it, the self does not develop properly. Further, authentic validation inoculates us from the ravages of shame. If we are receiving adequate amounts of authentic validation, then shameful comments or feelings simply have little impact on us. After all, if others are providing authentic validation, what do we have to feel shameful about?

> "I get so tired of faking it. I know that's a strong word 'fake' but it's absolutely how I feel. I've never liked going to the gym. Most cocktail parties bore me silly. I'm a fish-out-of-water at most gay bars. Honestly, I'd rather sit at home and eat bad food and watch bad TV with a boyfriend who likes to do the same."
>
> NICK FROM JACKSONVILLE, FL

Without the inoculating effects of authentic validation, shame is debilitating. It is a hugely powerful emotion that is very distressing. It causes us to immediately withdraw and try to hide. We want to cover up our mistakes and run away.

Because shame is so distressing, we are highly motivated to avoid feeling it. There are two tactics we can use to avoid shame, and we often use them both. The first tactic is to avoid situations that evoke feelings of shame (e.g., not returning the call of a friend who criticized you). The second tactic is to elicit validation to compensate for the shame (e.g., flirting with another man after having a fight with your boyfriend). Later, we will discuss in detail the ways in which we use both of these "shame-fighting" tactics to protect ourselves against the emotional ravages of shame.

With an inability to self-generate authentic validation, to feel good just because we are who we are, we walk through the world feeling frequently invalidated. At times, we see it everywhere: at home, with our lover, at work, or just walking the street. Even the most minor slight can be perceived as invalidation.

This reminds me of a client who once said to me, "Tom (his lover) told me that he really liked the dinner I made, and afterwards, all I could think of is 'he must have really disliked my other meals.'" When we are vulnerable to invalidation, we tend to find it in places where it does not exist.

Because we are very vulnerable to shame and because it is triggered so easily within us, our lives become solely focused on avoiding shame and seeking validation. Almost everything becomes either an avoidance strategy or an invitation for validation.

For the young gay man, his life often becomes obsessed with avoiding shame. He attempts to avoid situations that evoke shame or increase the validation he is receiving. The young gay man avoids gym class (where the other boys make fun of him), and he becomes a straight-A student to achieve some validation. Or perhaps he surrounds himself with friends (mostly girls) who don't seem to notice or care that he is different, and he achieves validation by wearing the most up-to-date and stylish clothes. Or he attempts to become "hypermasculine" by working out at the gym and becoming the star athlete so that no one suspects the real truth about him. One common thread runs through all of these examples: *The avoidance of shame becomes the single most powerful, driving force in his life.*

The consequence of this is that his true self remains undeveloped and hidden deep within him. Who he is, what he really likes, his true passion, and more are all colored and buried beneath the façade he has developed to avoid shame. While this helps him to cope with the distress and subsequent avoidance of shame, it is a recipe for trouble in life. At first, the trouble is seemingly minor, but as he grows older he becomes increasingly aware that he doesn't really know what he wants out of life and what might make him ultimately fulfilled and content. As the years go by, his awareness of this deficit grows, causing various maladies including deepening depression, conflictual and faltering relationships, substance abuse, and sleepless anxiety.

Chapter 3

OUT & RAGING

By the time the gay boy becomes a man, he is well-practiced in the art of achieving validation for his actions that may be praiseworthy, but are inauthentic to him. He is, so to speak, a validation junky. He moves from friend to friend, lover to lover, job to job, and city to city seeking the nectar he craves. Make no mistake about it, he is driven in his quest.

For some gay men, the quest takes him into more traditional roles. He finds a mate and makes a home. He seeks validation through the traditional veins that his father mined, albeit with the opposite sex. A good job, a beautiful home, lavish holidays, and exotic vacations are the tools he uses. He may augment his exploration with adopted children, a home in the country or on the beach, and even a prestigious position at the local church or synagogue. All of these are laudable and socially valuable pursuits, but the gay man who does so solely in the pursuit of validation is never satisfied, no matter how good he is at these endeavors. All he accomplishes satisfies for only a passing moment before the relentless hunger for more that is better burns once again.

Other gay men seek validation through sexual conquest and adoration. If this is you, you'll spend most of your spare time at the gym, building what you believe is the body that will one day earn you enough adoration to satisfy your craving for it. You keep score meticulously, noting each and every admirer who might throw a ravishing glance your way.

"I met Shane on bigmuscle.com. He was the hottest man I'd ever seen,—every muscle was ripped from his head to his toes. It surprised me that sex with Shane was never really that good, once I got over my fascination with his body. It was like he was always onstage and could never really let himself go and enjoy it."

CHARLES FROM CHICAGO, IL

The stories are varied and mixed, but the outcome is the same. The gay man who isn't able to believe in himself, to be satisfied with himself, seeks validation from the world around him, but he finds what validation that he does receive increasingly fails to satisfy.

Unable to satisfy his own needs, feelings of rage begin to emerge. His tolerance for invalidation becomes dangerously low and his hunger for validation is all-consuming. Sometimes, even the smallest of perceived slights ignites a flash of red-hot anger within him: The catered brunch isn't flawless and he explodes at the caterer. The business partner fails to fully execute his directives, the client is lost, and he explodes with a self-righteous fury. His lover no longer lavishes him with praise, and he withdraws into an angry emotional shell, and perhaps seeks out an affair in retribution.

The rage he feels is the natural, emotional outcome of being placed into an impossible dilemma. Nothing he does solves the enigmatic riddle that plagues him. He is driven by a hunger for validation, yet when he achieves it, the feeling is emptiness. The harder he tries, the less he is satiated. More and better yields only less and worse. Nothing he does seems to really change the forces that pin him to the mat. No amount of struggle, wriggling, even retreat makes a difference.

Rage is the experience of intense anger that results from his failing to achieve authentic validation. Since authentic validation can occur only in the context of one's true, authentic self, he finds himself incapable of achieving the one thing that will bring him lasting contentment. Like a cornered and terrified animal, he is provoked, snarling and demanding that he be set free from the cage to which he has been leashed.

Of course, his rage only pushes others away, and the sacred validation that he craves goes with them. So he hides his anger in the velvet glove, quickly returning to the gracious friend and lover he aspires to be.

Life, then, becomes an ever vacillating seesaw between rage and gentility. He reaches out to his world for validation, always sensitive to the slightest invalidation to which he responds with swift rage.

INHIBITED RAGE AND SHAME

Josh was extremely bright. At thirty-five, he was an Ivy League MBA graduate and very successful marketing executive. He came to therapy because of depression and loneliness.

Josh had been in several intense, long-term relationships. Each had followed a different course but the similarities were all too familiar. In each relationship, Josh would start to feel invalidated by his lover: He wasn't getting enough attention, the lover wasn't interested enough in sex, the lover was more interested in his friends than Josh, etc. Finally the day would come when Josh had

had all he could take. A big blow-up would follow and the lover would move out.

Josh adamantly denied feeling any rage. Sure, he would admit to having been angry during fights with his lovers, but on the whole he saw himself as a very compassionate, tender human being.

Months later, Josh came into therapy reporting that his depression had worsened upon receiving the recent news that he hadn't been promoted to a district vice-presidential position he wanted. The feedback from his boss was that Josh was too difficult as a supervisor. Too many of his employees—some apparently very qualified—had quit because they found Josh too demanding. Josh spent much of that therapy session venting about how wrong his boss was, and how unfair it was that feedback from disgruntled employees had been used to deny him the promotion.

What happened in Josh's case is similar to what happens for many of us. Because he has spent most of his life successfully avoiding shame—academic and business success being just a few of the tactics he used—he hadn't felt the debilitating onslaught of shame for years. That is, not until now. The denial of the promotion was the battering ram that broke through his brittle defenses and allowed the shame to come flooding in. Josh was drowning in his shame, to the point where he was even considering suicide.

Josh's story illustrates a monumental problem gay men experience. Because we learned at a very young age to successfully avoid shame, we don't often experience the shame in its full intensity. Our avoidance tactics keep the shame at bay, until like with Josh, we are hit by the force of an intense invalidation.

Marc was a client who came to therapy seeking help for a relationship that was falling apart. Quite unrelated to his treatment goal, I happened to discover that Marc had not flown in an airplane for more than fifteen years. He had plenty of opportunity to fly, but had always managed an excuse not to do so. While it was quite clear to me that Marc had a phobia of flying, when I asked him about it, he said, "I don't really think that I'm afraid to fly. I used to be terrified at the thought of it, but now I actually think I could do it if I wanted to."

Marc had avoided flying for so many years that he actually had convinced himself that he wasn't afraid to fly. Because he hadn't exposed himself to the experience of flying and his intense fear of it for many years, it seemed to him that he was no longer afraid to fly. One can only imagine that putting plane tickets in his hand and driving him to the airport would bring all the fear and anxiety rushing back.

What both Josh and Marc experienced were *inhibited emotions*. Inhibited emotions are those feelings that we successfully avoid and therefore don't feel. Josh hadn't felt shame for years, and if you had asked him prior to losing the promotion if shame was a problem for him, he'd probably have laughed at the idea. Marc hadn't experienced the intense phobic anxiety in years, too, since he had carefully avoided flying. Despite the fact that both of these men hadn't felt the emotion they were avoiding regularly, their lives were still significantly shaped by them. Sometimes inhibited emotions influence our lives more than emotions we feel.

Inhibited emotions, especially rage and shame, are a major problem for gay men. We don't *feel* the shame and rage, so we aren't aware how significantly these emotions are affecting and influencing our lives. The truth is that the *avoidance* of shame and rage, as much as the actual experiencing of these emotions, troubles us.

If we don't *feel* shame and rage, how do we know that we are avoiding them? First, on the occasions that we do feel the shame and rage, we feel them with an intensity that is beyond what the circumstance merits. In other words, we tend to overreact. Secondly, we haven't developed the skills to tolerate these emotions when they do occur—strongly suggesting that we have been avoiding shame and rage for quite some time. The end result is that they can have debilitating effects.

"I remember my first boyfriend used to just fly into a rage at the least little thing. Normally, he was a quiet, nice guy, but underneath that boy-next-door exterior was a raging bull. Say the wrong thing at just the wrong time, and watch out! He got so angry at me one time that he threw a chair through a plate glass window."

ART FROM AUSTIN, TX

In our everyday lives, we may be aware of occasional anger resulting from the ordinary frustrations, but it's not obvious that this anger is truly rage. However, a closer look shows the evidence of rage all around us. To begin with, gay men are known for a cynical and biting sense of humor. We often use humor as a channel for our rage. No one can write a searing commentary on the latest fashion faux pas of a celebrity like a gay man. Society has come to recognize and appreciate the sharp-tongued, "bitchy" humor of gay men.

Another sign of our rage is the speed and intensity with which our anger is sometimes ignited. Gay men have often been known to become furious over the smallest issue. It can be some off-hand comment or insignificant detail that triggers our anger at lightning speed. I often hear it said among psychotherapists who treat gay men that one of the primary problems troubling gay male relationships seeking couple's therapy is this hypersensitivity to invalidation and the ensuing flight into anger.

I once heard this called the crash and lash syndrome, a phrase that I've adopted because it really captures the expression of a gay man's rage. A verbal slight, an off-hand insult, a glimpse of a disapproving face—any of these things have been known to trigger the crash and lash syndrome of rage. The crash occurs when we are overwhelmed with rage, and all rational thought comes to an abrupt halt. The emotion seems to erupt within us, consuming us and overloading our brains with thoughts steeped in shame and anger. Then, in a matter of seconds, we lash out at the person who triggered the rage within us. Sometimes, when we are able to stop ourselves from lashing out, we simply retreat, mulling over the distress and sinking deeper into the emotion.

The crash and lash of rage became clear to Josh as we worked together in therapy. Although at first he clung to the idea that he had been the perfect supervisor, over time he began to talk about the ways in which he had been extraordinarily quick to criticize others. Sometimes he would hold back his anger. At other times, he would descend on his employees with the full power of his position of authority and correct them publicly.

The more Josh became aware of his rage, the more he learned about himself and his behavior. He began to notice the connection between periods when he felt especially invalidated and his temper flares. Often, he discovered, the anger he expressed at employees was in fact misdirected. The employees learned early on to always validate Josh, but they quickly became the target for the rage caused by an invalidation Josh experienced elsewhere.

Rage as an emotion has an identifying characteristic: like anger, it always seeks a target. Very often the target for rage isn't the real source of the invalidation but some other convenient person within our environment. The slow checker at the grocery store or the person who accidentally cuts us off on the freeway becomes the undeserved recipient of the fury of our anger.

While rage can certainly have many forms, all take aim at two kinds of targets. The first target is those around us. The second is ourselves, by internalizing the rage through self-hatred and depression. These two outcomes of rage affect our lives immeasurably.

When we target our rage on those around us, we inevitably push them away, creating an environment of mistrust and confusion in our relationships. Over time, we find our inner circle of friendship is always in a state of flux, with most close relationships lasting only a few years, at best. Other people can tolerate our rage for only so long before they are forced to walk away to protect their own self-esteem. In the event that the relationship involves another gay man who also strikes out in rage, the relationship is almost immediately volatile and unstable.

> "I reached a point where I honestly didn't care if I got HIV or not. Actually, it was a relief when I found out I was finally positive."
>
> BART FROM NEW YORK, NY

On the other hand, when we focus our rage internally, we do even greater damage. Internalized rage manifests in self-defeating patterns of behavior: substance abuse, reckless disregard for safe sex and HIV, financial irresponsibility, career dropout, and repeatedly destroying the opportunities for success that come our way.

Rage is the mortal enemy of gay men everywhere. It can arrive under a cloak of secrecy, and with amazing speed it consumes our lives. Because we often don't recognize it for what it truly is, we invite it into our lives, feed it, nurture it, and give ourselves wholly over to it. Not until we've paid a great price, do most of us begin to see it for the dark enemy that it is.

STAGE 1: OVERWHELMED BY SHAME

"If we are not ashamed to think it, we should not be ashamed to say it."

MARCUS TULLIUS CICERO
(106BC – 43BC)

Chapter 4

DROWNING

It was Mitch's mother who first came to see me. She was distraught. Before she sat down in my office, the tears were welling in her eyes. "I just don't know what to do anymore. No matter what I do or say, he just gets so *angry*."

Mitch's mother was no stranger to suffering. She'd been married and widowed in her forties, lost one child who was only two years old, and had just recently been given the "complete remission" prognosis from her doctor after a ten-year battle with ovarian cancer. Despite all the trauma and suffering, she wasn't self-pitying or bitter. Suffering seems to make some people ever so victimized, and others, like Mitch's mom, it makes them softer, more compassionate. She said that all she wanted was for her sons to be happy, and she said it with such conviction that I couldn't help but believe her. She was the mother of three sons, two of whom were identical twins, Mitch and Martin. Martin was gay and had been out of the closet for three years, since his twenty-fifth birthday. Mitch, on the other hand, had a girlfriend.

For many years, Mitch had been unable to keep a job for more than a year or two. Time and again, he had become explosively

angry and quit in a rage or was fired. His relationships, too, had
been stormy. Not all that long ago, his current girlfriend had actually acquired a restraining order against him because of his
volatile behavior.

During the past year, Mitch had become impossible with his
family. All it took was the slightest comment or criticism, and
he stormed out of the house. Or worse, he'd slam the door to
his garage apartment (it was attached to his mother's house)
and drink himself into a stupor. Mitch's mother didn't know
what to do. Life with Mitch had become so miserable that she
was seriously considering kicking him out of the apartment.
Everyone in the family, including Martin, thought it was past
time that she do it.

In the year that followed, I saw Mitch's mother occasionally as
she needed to talk over her concerns about the family. During
that year, Mitch continued to spin out of control. When he lost
his job at one of the local high-tech plants, he drove his car to the
Bay Bridge that connects Oakland with San Francisco and
jumped off. Inside the car, he left a note that read, in part, "I'd
rather be dead than be gay."

Mitch's story is so tragic, and yet it's probably fair to say that
most gay men have had similar feelings at some point early in
their lives. It would be better not to be alive than to be gay. Of
course, most of us didn't act on that feeling, but nonetheless, we
are no stranger to that lonely desperation.

Even though we may not have been suicidal, most—if not all—
gay men start at this place of being overwhelmed with the shame
of being gay in a world that worships masculine power. This begins
the first of three stages in a gay man's life, and it is the stage that is
characterized by being *overwhelmed by shame*. This is the start of
his journey as a gay man, and it is by far the most difficult and

damaging. He'd do anything not to be gay. He suffers immensely the pain of knowing that he can't change the one thing that makes him so different from other men. He imagines that being gay will ruin his life completely, and *there is nothing he can do to change it.*

During stage one, the shame over being gay reaches a loud crescendo. He knows there is something horribly wrong with himself and is helpless to change it. No amount of dating girls, playing straight, or even wishing changes it. Like Mitch, he is faced with the undeniable reality that he is irreversibly gay.

> "The irony is that I would have done anything not to be gay. My dad said, 'I can't believe you're doing this.' And I said: 'I can't believe it either.'"
>
> CHRISTIAN FROM AKRON, OH

Coping in stage one means finding a way—*any way*—to lessen the feeling of shame. Very soon he discovers that shame is manageable if he learns to avoid the cues in his world that trigger the intolerable feeling. In no time, he is about the business of avoiding all manner of situations, people, and feelings that trigger his sense of shame.

In stage one, there are many ways to avoid experiencing the toxic shame of being gay. One of the more drastic methods of avoidance, as Mitch chose, is suicide. Suicide among gay men in stage one is shockingly common. One study found that homosexual (whether out or not) males account for more than half of male youth suicide attempts. Another study of ninety-five gay and bisexual men between the ages of fifteen and twenty-six found that fifty-four percent of these men had seriously considered suicide compared to only thirteen percent of men in the general population.

These and many other research statistics bear out a similar story—young gay men struggle desperately with their sexuality during the early years of their adult lives. These are the years when stage one is most acute, and we haven't yet learned more functional ways to avoid the devastating aspects of shame. We are slammed head-on with shame, and it feels overwhelming, and to many, mortally unbearable.

Most of us, however, found a less drastic way than suicide to avoid shame. The first, and undoubtedly the most common way we avoided shame, was to deny our sexuality. We simply acted as if we weren't gay. After all, our logic went, if we didn't act gay, maybe we weren't.

DENIAL OF SEXUALITY

While denying our sexuality, we may have become hypersexual with women, needing to always have the most beautiful, sexy woman we could find on our arm. We denied our attraction to men and attempted to convince ourselves and everyone else that we were really straight—or at a minimum bisexual.

Gay men who actively deny their sexuality, even for a brief period of time, also usually distance themselves from anything that appeared remotely gay. During my own stage one, I got married to a woman in what I can now see was a desperate effort to deny my true sexuality. During that time in my life, I avoided my wife's brother, who was quite obviously gay. It seemed to me at the time that if I hung around my wife's brother, others would see the similarities between us and discover my secret.

Many gay men who are in denial of their sexuality gravitate to strong, anti-gay activities and organizations. Venture into any church that preaches a strong anti-gay message, and you're guaranteed to find more than a small sample of gay men who are actively in denial of their sexuality. Or visit just about any fire-house where the firemen are regularly throwing around words like "faggot" and "homo" to insult their buddies, and you might well find a gay fireman who is desperately struggling to deny his homoerotic feelings.

When a gay man is in denial of his sexuality, it is often very perplexing to those around him. Whether or not his family and friends have figured out that he is gay, they are confused, even dumbfounded, by the odd inconsistencies in his behavior. He may become suddenly depressed and sullen, and speak momentarily of "dark secrets" that haunt him, without revealing the content of those secrets. He may become explosively angry at the least provocation. Should anyone come close to suggesting he is gay, he is likely to become enraged and strike out at the person who had the misfortune of uncovering his sexual feelings.

> "Years later I learned that practically every guy in the youth choir at church was gay. None of us admitted it at the time because we either didn't want to be gay or because if we were, we'd have been kicked out. In that church, being gay was a 'go-straight-to-hell' lifestyle."
>
> LENNY FROM DALLAS, TX

Many supportive families have discovered the hazards of exposing a gay man's sexuality when he is in denial. Thinking that they are being helpful, even loving, they may attempt to confront him in the spirit of making him comfortable with sharing his sexuality, only to receive in return a barrage of anger and denial.

I remember seeing one couple in therapy after they had asked their eighteen-year-old son if he was gay. They had carefully explained to him that if he were gay, it was fine by them and that they only wanted him to be happy. The son angrily exploded at them saying, "You've never had a clue who I am," hurriedly packed a backpack, and left the house. By the time they saw me, he hadn't returned for over a week.

When we were denying that we were gay, we *acted as if* we were straight. "Acting as if" meant that we had to split our lives into two parts: One part was the acceptable, public self. The other part was the secretive, darker self. The darker self learned to meet men on the sly—at the mall, on business trips, in the park, on the internet, in the locker room, or at the highway rest stop. We had sex, often without exchanging real names (after all, we couldn't afford for some screaming queen to tell our secret all about town). We convinced ourselves that we weren't gay, just playing around with a guy until the right girl came along. However we justified it, *we definitely weren't gay.* We were bisexual, curious, and damned horny. What's so wrong with two guys taking care of business?

Some gay men in stage one don't act out their secret fantasy life. Instead of seeking "secret" sex, they harbor elaborate erotic fantasies about sex with men. These fantasies commonly grow so strong that the gay man becomes phobic of ever acting out the fantasy for fear of losing control. One client said it well: "I knew if I ever allowed myself to have sex with a man, the dam would break, and I'd never be able to go back to sex with my wife."

The damaging effect of learning to live your life in two parts, whether in reality or fantasy, cannot be underestimated. It is an infectious skill that you learned, one that would eventually spread beyond the bedroom of your life. Life wasn't ever what it seemed on the surface. Nothing could be trusted for what it appeared to be. After all, you weren't what you appeared to be. In learning to hide part of yourself, you lost the ability to trust anything or anyone fully. Without knowing it, you traded humane innocence for dry cynicism.

Splitting, as this is known, is especially problematic. For many of us, long after we stop hiding the fact that we are gay, we continue to split off unacceptable parts of ourselves. We present a rosy picture of our relationship to coworkers, or we feign enjoyment at the dinner party thrown by a wealthy acquaintance just because it might increase our social status. Who we really are and what we truly feel is something very different from what we display for others in that moment.

While you may be thinking that this is just plain old dishonesty, it is in reality a much deeper psychological issue. It's about living dishonestly, faking an entire segment of our lives for the benefit of getting along in life. Even more troubling, when we are actively splitting we generally don't think of ourselves as being dishonest.

Ken is a case in point. Only after many years of therapy did he come clean about the extensive, second life he was living via the internet. At night, on weekends, and during breaks in the day, he would chat on the internet with the intention of arranging a sexual hook-up. Over a few years previous to his disclosure, he estimated that he had sex with probably more than a hundred different men. At the same time, Ken had been in a relationship with another man, Dave, who lived in another state. While they hadn't committed to monogamy yet, it was clear to Ken that his boyfriend was monogamous. In fact, Ken had artfully dodged the discussion of monogamy so as to avoid being cornered into a commitment he knew he would have to make to keep the relationship.

When disclosing his second life on the internet, Ken said, "I could never tell Dave about this. He would be so hurt. What would be the point if I stop it now?" Of course, the truth of the situation was that more than protecting Dave's feelings (which would surely have been very hurt), Ken was obviously mostly protecting *himself* from the shame of having lived a dual life.

Splitting is undoubtedly the most troublesome and persistent behavior learned during stage one, and it often lingers long after you've left stage one. When you split, you are able, if only temporarily, to avoid shame. If your boyfriend doesn't know about the affair, you aren't confronted with shame. If your coworkers don't know you're gay, you won't risk being treated like you're part of the "out group." If your parents are never allowed to visit your one-bedroom apartment, they might not find out that your boyfriend is living with you.

> "The internet was the best thing that ever happened to my sex life. I could meet guys for sex and never tell them my real name or address. It's a gay married man's heaven."
>
> CHARLES FROM
> HATTIESBURG, MS

While splitting often allows us to avoid shame, it also eventually undermines our relationships. We are never what we appear to be, and over time, others begin to sense this. Trust erodes from our relationships with lovers, friends, and family. We are marginalized and kept at a safe distance by others. In any case, they discover that they don't really know us at all. How can they trust someone they don't even know?

Splitting, as significant as it is, is just one of the ways in which we learn to avoid shame while in stage one. Let me tell you the story of Travis.

I met Travis after he entered an alcohol rehabilitation treatment center that often referred gay male patients to me. All of seventeen years old, he was already experiencing regular blackouts and painful withdrawal whenever he didn't drink. A quart of hard liquor a day had become his habit.

Travis always knew that he was different from the other boys. To start with, he was always smaller and developmentally behind the boys of his age. He loved to play the piano and had absolutely no interest in sports. While he enjoyed the company of girls, at twelve years old he knew that he was mostly attracted to other boys.

Travis's father suspected that he was gay. He was a very controlling man who had spent nearly twenty years as a practicing alcoholic before he finally gave up drinking. After that, he seemed to become even more difficult and angry, especially toward Travis. At our first meeting, Travis had a broken arm and numerous bruises from the last beating his father had given him. But these were only the visible wounds; his father had also called him a "God damn faggot," "cock sucker," and "fairy," standard insults that he flung at Travis when he became the least bit angry. Travis's response was to run away from home; he'd done so many times before, living on the streets for weeks at a time.

As we worked together, Travis was able to identify the intense shame he felt for being different. Although he hated those hateful words that his father flung at him, deep inside he had come to believe they were true. Underneath it all, he felt worthless.

For Travis, alcohol was a way to avoid the intense shame he had internalized from his father. In fact, most of his binges had occurred after he had fights with his father. Despite his deep anger toward him, there was a part of Travis that still revered his father and believed that he was right.

After being able to maintain sobriety for several months while in the treatment program, Travis began reporting intense feelings of shame, hopelessness, and a desire to isolate himself from the other boys in the treatment center. The other residents were all straight, and he was certain that they looked down on him.

The only way Travis could handle his shame was to drink. Of course, the treatment center had taken away his one effective avoidance strategy, and he was left helpless to fight his demons without his usual weaponry.

Substance abuse is a common avoidance strategy that many gay men learn at this early stage of the struggle to cope with the trauma of being gay in a straight man's world, and consequently, it is an epidemic among gay men. All the research confirms it, and if you've spent any time in a large city's gay neighborhood, you've seen it, too. Everything from alcohol to cocaine to ecstasy to heroin. It's all there, and regularly being lapped up by party boys and muscle daddies alike. Try to imagine a gay nightclub where at least half the people weren't stoned, drunk, or tripping on ecstasy—it's hard to do.

Clearly, substance abuse is one of the ways some of us learned to avoid shame. In fact, for some of us, it is the *only* way we learned to avoid shame. If we could get high enough for long enough, we could forget the shame that dogs us throughout the day. Only then could we let go and really have a good time.

I work with many gay men who have come to believe that they can't have sex unless they are high or intoxicated. The only way they can let go is to medicate themselves out of the shame. Shame is insidious and ubiquitous, and the need to avoid it is equally ever-present, especially when we are bare-naked and vulnerable with another man.

Substance abuse isn't just a circuit-party-going queen's issue, either. I've rarely been to a dinner party hosted by gay men where alcohol wasn't flowing generously. A cocktail or two before dinner, bottles of wine with dinner, and aperitifs afterwards are not unusual. Recently, I attended a dinner party where two separate guests each arrived with a large bottle of liquor for their own cocktails. Apparently, the host was known for not keeping a very well-stocked bar.

Still another way gay men avoid shame is in anonymous sex. It's quick, easy, no ties, no names. After all, if you don't know his name, you have a great excuse never to call or talk to him again. When a man gets to know you intimately, he becomes uniquely equipped to point out your flaws and shortcomings. By limiting yourself to brief sexual encounters with a man you know only superficially at best, you get all the goodies and none of the other stuff. It's just quick, clean, honest fun—or so we tell ourselves. How honest can a brief encounter truly be?

All of us know a gay man, maybe even ourselves, who intentionally has only brief relationships with other men. Just as soon as the relationship starts to feel committed, we find a reason to break it off or to drive the other person out of our life. All it takes is an inkling of shame, and we're on the run.

These brief relationships may whet our sexual appetite, but they do little to gain us authentic, self-generated validation. Hence, they also do little to dampen our rage. The consequence of all this is that the more short-lived relationships and sexual encounters we have, the more cynical we become about relationships. After all, none of our relationships has come close to satisfying the ravenous yearning for authentic validation. We can become critical and easily angered in even brief relationships as our rage grows and destroys our bond with those whom we also desire.

During stage one, we may also experience a great deal of compounded shame. Imagine this: You have a fight with your boyfriend, storm out of the house, and go down to the local gay bar, where you proceed to get smashed and do something to embarrass yourself. Maybe you dance on the bar in your underwear or perhaps you simply become obnoxious and loud. Whatever the behavior, you did something radical to try and silence the intense shame that the argument with your boyfriend ignited.

This is the nightmare of compounded shame, and we've all been there in one way or another. Compounded shame occurs when something triggers our shame, and we immediately go into avoidance mode, like storming out of the house and getting smashed at the bar. While we're pouring our heart and soul into avoidance, we suddenly discover that we're doing things that might be justifiably shameful, like singing naked on the piano bar.

"It was really stupid. I never even thought about having an affair. I was just trying to keep up with Jess, my lover, who was sleeping all over town. In the end, he left me when he found out that I'd been seeing a cute Puerto Rican guy on the side."

J.T. FROM NEW YORK, NY

Sometimes a powerful emotion like shame is followed by what is known as a secondary emotion. When shame is both the primary and the secondary emotion, this is called compounded shame. Other emotions, too, can be secondary to shame, such as anger or fear. For example, you become enraged with the person who "outed" you at the office, or you become overcome with the fear that your boyfriend will dump you. Shame often is the cue for other troubling emotions, creating a scenario where you go from feeling bad to much worse.

When I was in my very early twenties, I married a wonderfully talented woman named Karen. She was beautiful but had even more talent as a soprano. I mistakenly took our wonderful friendship as a sign of romance and decided that what I needed to do was to marry Karen. In time, I convinced myself that would be the solution to all my shame about being gay. In fact, it was going to cure me, and I wouldn't be gay anymore!

Of course, marrying didn't cure me of anything. Within two years, Karen and I were divorced. After the divorce, I struggled with dark feelings of shame, but this time it wasn't just about being gay. It was about being gay and having badly hurt a wonderful woman. For several years, I drowned in my compounded shame. The more shame I acknowledged, the more frantically I tried to avoid the shame. I used every possible escape hatch I knew to avoid the horrible feelings of guilt and shame. Early in my career I even abandoned my love of clinical work to climb the career ladder in human resources at Hewlett Packard, just to prove that I wasn't a scoundrel or some screaming queen. Maybe my sexuality wasn't conventional, but everything else about me was just fine.

Compounded shame and the associated rage is a toxic quagmire that can keep a gay man stuck in this uncomfortable, out-of-touch emotional stage for most of his life, until he comes to understand how shame is operating on him, feeding on him, controlling him, and keeping him from a more authentic life. As his shame confounds his relationship, job, and friendships, his frantic attempts to avoid shame increase in intensity. The splitting, dishonesty, substance abuse, and anonymous sex most surely increase, all in an attempt to pull himself out of the jaws of the shame that is consuming him. Those behaviors, in turn, eventually make him feel even more shameful, and on the cycle goes. This stage of a gay man's life is a truly devastating time. Some gay men move through it quickly while others linger, and some even spend an entire lifetime suffering the torment of overwhelming shame. Regardless, this first stage often leaves us with several problematic coping behaviors, like splitting and shame avoidance. Romantic relationships created during this stage are almost always stormy and traumatic for both parties, and everyone is often deeply wounded by the experience.

Chapter 5

BEWITCHED, BETRAYED

The intimate relationships a gay man has while in stage one are often some of the most defining relationships of his life. It is a tumultuous time, filled with rage, fear, and shame. Confused about who he really is and what kind of life he might expect to have, he is often unpredictable, impulsive, and without clear direction. His relationships are often intense, explosive, and for so many gay men, deeply wounding.

Even as I write this chapter, my mind reels of my own lost relationships of those early years and the too-short relationships of my clients who often recount them through heavy tears of grief. In his 1995 autobiography *Palimpsest*, Gore Vidal—arguably the first openly gay male American novelist—tells of his tender, loving relationship with an astonishingly handsome man named Jimmie Trimble. Trimble's full-page picture in Vidal's book depicts an adolescent beauty; Vidal describes a lifelong infatuation with him.

Written by Vidal in his seventies, *Palimpsest* provides a sweeping and grand tour of his life. It's filled with references and bits of conversation with the rich, richer, and famous. He

tells of conversations with Jackie and Jack Kennedy, Charleton
Heston, Tennessee Williams, Marlon Brando, and Paul Bowles,
just to name a few of the luminaries with whom his life intertwined. And yet it is Jimmie Trimble who stands out from the
grandeur, a young man whom Vidal loved during his high
school years and who was killed in the World War II battle of
Iwo Jima at the tender age of nineteen. As Vidal states simply,
Trimble "was the unfinished
business of my life."[1] In the last
pages of his book, Vidal prints
the last picture taken of Jimmie
and in caption asks that he be
buried near Jimmie's grave.

> "Sometimes I think my first lover will be the only man I will ever really love. I would have given him everything I had . . . and eventually I did. I still think about him twenty years later."
>
> JORGE FROM SAN DIEGO, CA

What is it about a relationship with this young boy that so
imprinted itself upon Vidal's
life, a life that was lived between Hollywood, Washington, and
Europe among the most dashing and genteel of the times?
Why are gay men so affected by these early infatuations and
trysts? Why do so many of us go on to fill our lives with men
we can manage to forget?

The relationships formed in stage one have enormous power
over the gay man. That first experience of feeling romantic love
blended with erotic surge burns itself into our brains. The joy of
finally having touched the innermost secret and first feeling of
completeness it brings is monumental in our lives.

The darker side of stage one relationships is the overwhelming
shame that clouds and penetrates this first powerful relationship.
We are not free—not yet—and we struggle internally between
the two defining poles of our lives, shame and love. This emotional struggle manifests outwardly as intense relationships that

are often swiftly abandoned and subsequently denied, leaving one or both men stunned and heartbroken.

Michael told me the story of his first love, Phillip. He hadn't deliberately recalled the story for more than twenty years, and it was obvious as he told it that the memories and emotions were flooding back, at times reducing him to tears. Michael had met Phillip at the University of Texas during their sophomore year. At the time, they were dating two girls who were friends, and the foursome had quickly become an inseparable unit at football games and pizza parlors near the campus.

Michael remembered the first night that he began to feel something strangely attracting him to Phillip. The four of them returned to Phillip's apartment from a night out on the town. Behind the apartment was a pond, and Phillip suggested that they all go skinny-dipping. In a flash, they were all out on the lawn, stripping in the moonlight. Michael noticed the muscular curves of Phillip's body and the glistening of the small, blond hairs that covered most of his athletic torso. He also caught the sense that Phillip was noticing him, too. In the water they plunged, swimming, laughing, and playing. Michael remembers the feeling of arousal that haunted him that night, and the difficulty he had concealing his underwater erection.

As the months went by, Michael and Phillip began going out without their girlfriends in tow. What was once a delightfully unexpected encounter became a weekend ritual. The two would go out to a local bar and drink until they were both thoroughly drunk and then stumble back to Michael's place on the edge of campus. Drunk and pretending to not know what they were doing, the evening would culminate with the two men naked in bed making out. This ritual continued throughout their junior year. Michael recalls that year with great fondness and tells of how completely devoted he became to Phillip. He didn't think of either one of them as being gay, and yet he knew that he was completely taken with Phillip.

One night late in August before their senior year, Michael got a call from an old friend from high school who was obviously drunk. He asked Michael flat out if he was a homosexual. Phillip had been telling everyone around town that Michael had tried to seduce him, but Phillip had pushed him away and told him to go screw himself.

Now a strapping man in his forties, Michael shifted in his chair across from me and wept for several minutes. "I didn't know what to do. I just hung up the phone and thought I would die. I never spoke to Phillip again."

Michael told me of how he had replayed in his memory time and again how Phillip had caressed him, kissed him gently, and how the two of them often had half a dozen orgasms before dawn. Over and over again he scrutinized his memories, looking for any sign that Phillip had been an unwilling party to this or that his feelings for Phillip had been on false premises. There was nothing he could point to—he was sure that the feelings were mutual and that Phillip had been as much an initiator as he.

After this traumatic college experience, Michael had never been able to trust a lover again. He had great friends that he trusted completely, he said, but the minute he slept with a man, the suspicions raged. Michael desperately wanted a loving, long-term relationship but had come to believe that he was incapable of sustaining one. It was clear that his experience with Phillip, a man who so devilishly betrayed him some two decades earlier, stood in his way.

Like it was for both Gore Vidal and Michael, those early relationships created unprecedented emotional trauma that they subsequently carried into every succeeding relationship. For Vidal it was the young beauty who abandoned him through death, and for Michael it was the strong, athletic man who betrayed and publicly belittled him. Very different experiences, yet both affected these men for many years afterwards.

In this first stage of being a gay man, we are not equipped to have a healthy intimate relationship. Our own internal conflicts prevent us from gaining the emotional clarity needed to maintain a safe and satisfying bond. The situation compounds when two men, both overwhelmed with shame, come together in an intense and explosive expression of passion. What produces arguably the most erotic experiences of a gay man's life also takes him to the lowest place he is likely to know.

Many years ago in California, I treated Sean, a bright, very handsome young man who was in a residential treatment facility for adolescents. Sean had been placed into the facility for repeatedly running away from home and for frequent bouts of depression. When I met him, it became clear to both of us that Sean was gay. Although he described himself as bisexual, it was evident that his only real romantic feelings had been for other boys.

Sean told me that his maternal grandfather had been the only person who seemed to understand him. He was a wise old man who spent a great deal of time with Sean, taking him fishing and camping in the nearby mountains. These trips away from home were greatly welcomed respites from the frequent beatings he was subjected to by his stepfather. His mother had remarried when Sean was seven years old, and the stepfather had been determined to "whip him into shape."

I hadn't been treating Sean for very long when I learned that he had recently had a sexual affair with another male resident. Of course, sexual relations among any of the residents were strictly forbidden in treatment—the subsequent persecution brought from the other male residents was just one of the many good reasons why. The other boys whispered loud enough for Sean to hear "queer" and "homo" when he walked by. The taunting and embarrassment had become unbearable for Sean. The other resident with whom he had the affair denied having participated in anything and completely ignored Sean when the affair became public knowledge.

One Friday in July, I met with Sean just before he was to have a two-hour visit with his mother. He was so excited to see her and told me that he had convinced her that he was ready to return home now. As he told it, they were going to make plans for his discharge in the next week.

That Sunday, sitting out on the patio of my favorite coffee shop, my cell phone rang. The voice on the other end was frantic. "Dr. Downs, you've got to come to the office quickly." Concerned, I questioned the caller, a junior staff member at the facility, carefully. As he choked out the details, I started running to the car. One of the male residents had hanged himself.

On the drive to the treatment facility, I somehow knew that Sean was the person in question, but the staffer who had called me said that he wasn't sure. As I walked onto the grounds, I'll never forget what I saw. There, swinging from a rope tied to a tree not more than a hundred yards from my office, was Sean.

Nothing shakes you like having a client commit suicide. No amount of preparation or warnings from wise, experienced professors can prepare you for it. It makes you question everything about your profession, your skills, and the meaning of life.

What I took from this young man's suicide was a reverent awareness of the dire trauma that stage one relationships create.

I know that I will always be reminded of the significant and over-whelming consequences from these relationships. What casual observers might dismiss as young infatuations, I would always be careful to understand as powerful experiences that can become the template upon which many future relationships are built.

After his death, I learned that the visit with Sean's mother had gone poorly and that she had told him that he could not return be-cause his stepfather wouldn't allow a homosexual in the house. She told him he was to spend the next six months in treatment and hopefully "get over" his sexual problems. Undoubtedly, Sean had been drowned in overwhelming

> "Back in the '50s and '60s, it wasn't all that unusual to hear that a gay man had committed suicide. For a lot of men, it just wasn't an option to be a homo. It was just too disgraceful."
>
> DICK FROM OMAHA, NE

shame, not only from his parents but by a treatment center that had failed to keep him safe from the cruel tauntings of the other young men. It had been unbearable, and he chose the only es-cape he could think of.

Sean left behind two notes. One was to his mother telling her not to worry because he had gone to heaven to be with his beloved grandfather. And the other was addressed to me, apolo-gizing for having killed himself. He closed the note with these brief words scrawled in distressed handwriting: "You were the only one who understood."

My heart broke for Sean, and even now as I write these words I feel a bitter sorrow over a life needlessly wasted. My grief goes far beyond that brilliant boy who was so quickly snuffed out, to a world of gay men who have lived this trauma, too. To be gay in an uncompromisingly straight world is to struggle to find love and, once found, to hold on to it. We are men in a world where men are emotionally disabled by our masculine cultural ideals. And we are men who threaten those ideals by loving another man at a time in life when we are neither equipped for the ravishes of love or the torment of shame.

This early emotional stage is a traumatic and difficult time for all gay men. Those who grow up and live in a homophobic, invalidating environment usually suffer all the more. The memory of the struggle and the scars of the trauma are something we carry with us, long after we've moved on in life.

Chapter 6

THE REAL ME:

A CRISIS OF IDENTITY

The first stage of a gay man's development always culminates in a crisis of identity. Who am I? What direction will my life take? With whom will I identify myself? Who will I love? Eventually, no matter how hard we try to avoid it, the question, "Am I really gay?" demands an answer.

There are basically two ways in which we may resolve this crisis. One is to retreat into a permanent denial of our sexual preference, often referred to as "foreclosure." When a man forecloses on admitting he's gay, he gives up striving for authenticity. Of course, the other way to resolve this crisis of identity is to admit to our being gay and to make the choice to be openly gay. As perhaps you know, neither choice is completely easy. But peace of mind and being at peace with oneself doesn't come from foreclosure. No matter how hard it might be to be openly gay, it is the path toward being authentic.

During the crisis of identity, the drumbeat of shame beats louder and louder in the gay man's ears. Our emotions tend to vacillate from panic to deep sadness. We look at the world around us, the world of friends and acquaintances we have created for ourselves, and we imagine that very few of these people will accept us. We envision a lonely life, one that is childless and socially outcast. We believe that life as we have known it will completely collapse the day we announce we are gay.

Of course, you know that life doesn't collapse. Instead, life can take on a richness and added dimension of emotional depth that you can't imagine before taking the leap of coming out. But at the height of the crisis, we imagine this to be the only possible outcome. In the grinding grip of this crisis, many of us actually choose to retreat into a straight life in the hope of bringing relief from the suffocating shame that overwhelms us.

Donald had several male sexual relationships in college. He never publicly identified himself as gay and strongly preferred not to hang out with those who were openly gay. The few relationships he had with men were kept very private and superficial. Even after seeing one man for well over six months, the relationship was still more like one between acquaintances. He would meet his lover for the evening, have a few beers, have sex, and return home within a few hours. His lover was instructed to never leave a message on his home phone and absolutely never to acknowledge him in public should they accidentally meet.

After college, Donald returned to his hometown for a job that his father had secured for him at a local construction company. It wasn't too long afterward that his father's questions began: Who are you seeing these days? When will we have a wedding? Will I ever have grandchildren?

Donald had dated a number of different women in college, but none seriously. A date or two, maybe more, and he'd move on to another woman. On the golf course, he often complained to his father that he just couldn't find the right woman. Once settled in a job and new house, the pressure within him began to rise. Could he tell his family that he was really gay? Was he willing to throw everything away—as he imagined he would have to do—just for the chance to have sex with another man? The intense distress and anxiety kept him awake most nights until the early hours of the morning. What would he do?

Then he met Sharon. She was a beautiful woman whose family was very wealthy. And she seemed to really like him. Donald and Sharon dated steadily for two years, during which they grew quite close. They shared a lot of the same interests and dreams. At first, Donald found the sex to be interesting and even fun. But after awhile, it became something of a chore for him. Thankfully for Donald, Sharon didn't seem all that interested in sex herself.

It was about this time that Donald spotted a man named Kerry, walking through the lobby of the high-rise building where they both worked. The two exchanged a knowing glance, and Donald felt an old, familiar longing rising within him. In a day or two, Kerry struck up a conversation with Donald and eventually asked him out to dinner. They went to a very private, out-of-the-way restaurant of Donald's choosing, and ultimately made their way to Kerry's apartment. Then Donald did something he had never done before: He spent the whole night with a man.

When he returned home early the next morning, he was racked with guilt. What if Sharon had called during the night? What if there had been an emergency in the family and everyone was trying to find him? He was momentarily relieved when he checked the answering machine and saw there were no messages. He then phoned Sharon, who seemed to be her usual upbeat self. Thank goodness, he thought. He hadn't disclosed his secret.

Over the next weeks Donald found himself torn between erotic fantasies about Kerry and demoralizing guilt over Sharon. On two more occasions he arranged to be with Kerry, and after each time, the guilt and anguish over his lies to Sharon increased.

After weeks of sheer hell, losing weight and sleep, he decided to "fix it all" by asking Sharon to marry him. He did and she said yes. He told his plan to Kerry the next day over a very brief and nervous cup of coffee. Donald was flooded with relief and felt he had finally made a choice that would bring him peace and happiness.

As the years went on, Donald and Sharon had a baby boy. He was a very bright kid, and they found their lives consumed with caring for him and his insatiable curiosity of the world. But over these same years, Donald found himself slipping into a chronic, low-grade depression. His relationship with Sharon had cooled somewhat, although they were still kind and supportive of each other. He often felt that they were more like best friends who shared the same house and child.

When Donald finally came into my office for therapy, he was in his late forties and struggling with a worsening depression that had escalated when Sharon was diagnosed with multiple sclerosis. He imagined his future, and all he could see were endless trips with Sharon to the doctor, eventually visiting her in a nursing home, and ultimately putting their son through college by himself. Life had become an agonizing burden.

It was well over a year before Donald even hinted to me that he had had relationships with men when he was much younger. Even though he often found himself privately reviewing these memories with erotic zeal, he had not revealed them to another living soul. In the cocoon of the therapy office and on a particularly difficult day, he told it all. He was quick to add that he was not gay, and that he wished that I would leave all of this out of my notes. I agreed, and he left the office seeming a bit relieved but anxious at having told someone his shameful secret.

Donald was never able to allow himself to come out as gay, although in the privacy of his therapist's office he was finally able to admit that he probably was so. Too much of life was built on the façade he had created, and he dared not destroy it. Not surprisingly, his depression lifted only slightly during his work in therapy, but he eventually quit therapy, resigned to the idea that his life was already set before him, and there was nothing he could do about it.

Whereas he might have come out to his family and started living an authentic and honest life, Donald foreclosed on his crisis of identity. He felt immediate relief at having made a decision, but the decision led to long-term distress. Men like Donald often come to therapy in their thirties and older, having no clue as to why they are depressed, anxious, and having difficulty in their marriages. They inevitably see themselves as "nice guys" who have been treated unfairly, either by specific individuals or, as in Donald's case, by fate itself. Most often, they have little insight into the connection between unfulfilled sexual yearnings and their current distress. Some are able to work this through and eventually allow themselves to explore the side of life they had earlier forbid themselves to taste. Unfortunately, almost as many others refuse to make this journey, and instead, blame everyone else including themselves for their unhappiness. And they fundamentally cling to the belief that they are not gay.

Foreclosing on the crisis of identity has destroyed more men's lives than can be counted. While obviously the majority of men are not gay, there is a sizable minority of men who have chosen a straight life despite their sexual preference for men. They hang out at the gym and other places where men go, stealing a quick glance now and again. They notice men, and just as quickly turn away their attention so the delicate balance they've set up in their lives is not disturbed by a forbidden desire.

HOMOPHOBIC STRAIGHT MEN

While most straight men simply repress any homoerotic feelings, there are some men who are so distressed by these feelings that they become belligerent toward any man who triggers such unacceptable sexual feelings. More than just passively foreclosing on their identify crisis, these men actively create a violent heterosexual identity. They throw pejoratives around such as "cocksucker" and "faggot." When they want to attack another person verbally, they march out the list of nasty, homophobic words and phrases.

"My father was definitely a J. Edgar Hoover type. He hated himself because he was attracted to men and hated even more men who allowed themselves to indulge their pleasures. He was always making some comment about 'the God damn homos.'"

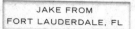

JAKE FROM
FORT LAUDERDALE, FL

Adolescent boys commonly engage in homophobic verbal attacks, as they are engorged with hormones that stir up all manner of feelings. This is unfortunate but normal, since our culture places such a high value on masculinity-over-femininity ideal, and homosexuality is viewed as the ultimate betrayal of this unspoken cultural value. In high school and college, most boys grow out of the need to be homophobic and relegate homosexuality to the list of subjects that they rarely, if ever, discuss.

Those young men who struggle with strong attractions to other men don't tend to outgrow the need to attack that which they don't fully understand. They continue to attack homosexuality, as the whole subject causes them great distress. They are shamed by their innermost feelings and fantasies, and that shame quickly transforms into rage that is directed toward eliminating homoerotic feelings. The target of their rage becomes men who have, in their opinions and through a deep character flaw, allowed themselves to become homosexual.

When a gay man forecloses on his crisis of identity, and represses his feelings in an attempt to live a straight life, his distress is immense. This becomes the root of depression or other ailments, and if not resolved, can grow into a variety of chronic and troubling psychological symptoms.

The gay man who resolves his crisis of identity and comes to honest terms with his sexual attraction to men is the man who will resolve his depression. He begins to explore what it means to live in a predominantly straight world. For the first time in his life, he no longer hides that tender part of himself from the rest of the world.

When you confront your crisis of identity and face the truth of who you really are, life begins to take on an entirely new look. Old friends who aren't comfortable with you being gay begin to fall away. A few might reject you immediately, and others slowly drift away. At the same time, you form a network of gay men and gay-friendly others. Often in short order, your relationships begin to reshape around those who are accepting of who you really are.

As you move from living in the closet to being out about your sexuality, the desire grows within you once again to silence the shame that once overwhelmed you. This time, rather than being subjugated by your feeling of shame, you begin to attack it vigorously, attempting to prove to yourself that you are worthwhile and loveable as a gay man.

While there is great relief from finally revealing the secret of your true sexuality, another internal tug-of-war begins to churn within you. You feel compelled to become the best, most successful, beautiful, and creative man you can be. You lurch forward into life, leaving achievement and creativity strewn in your path. You must prove to the world that you are no longer shameful. It is at this juncture in life, torn between the shame of your sexuality and a burning rage at the world that made you feel shameful, that you enter the second stage of the gay man's journey.

STAGE 2:
COMPENSATING
FOR SHAME

"Nothing succeeds like the appearance of success."

CHRISTOPHER LASCH

Chapter 7

PAYING THE PIPER

I have very fond memories of Napa Valley. During the years when I lived in San Francisco, I spent many weekends at the house of a good friend and his lover, atop a mountain just above the small village of St. Helena in the valley. We'd often race over the Golden Gate Bridge just as soon as we could leave work on Friday afternoon, making the hour-and-a-half trek to the spectacular Santa Fe–style adobe home that my friends had built.

The house was nothing less than a showplace. It had been photographed many times and published in both local and national interior design magazines. The walls were more than a foot and a half thick, filled with the mud adobe bricks that kept the house warm in the winter and cool in the summer from nothing more than the mountain breeze. The pool seemed to cantilever over the valley, and when floating across its glassy water, it was as if you were drifting just above the clouds and the scattered hot air balloons that often traversed the valley several hundred feet below the elevation of the house.

Dinners at the house in Napa were always lavish affairs. Nothing was ever simple or easy. The fish was always fresh and exotic, while the pies were always handmade and topped with generous scoops of gourmet delights. My friends always insisted on having the best of everything. They were—and are—wonderful hosts.

During my many visits, we were often joined by other gay men who had weekend homes in the valley. They were surgeons, corporate lawyers, investment bankers, and winemakers. Not one of them was anything less than outrageously successful in his chosen profession.

Back at work in the corporate offices of my high-tech company, my straight friends marveled at the continuous parade of the fabulous and famous dinner companions I kept on the weekends. I delighted in regaling them with my stories of the multi-millionaire investment banker, who happened to be a passenger with his lover on a Hawaiian Air jet that nearly disintegrated in air and landed without a roof over the passenger compartment. As if he weren't wealthy enough, he had sued the airline for untold millions and won. This he told us, with a chuckle and a clink of a wineglass, was how he paid for the five-mile paved road that was the private driveway to his mountaintop mansion in the valley (he also owned virtually the entire mountain). My straight coworkers would shake their heads in amazement as they recalled their own weekend of eating out at the Olive Garden or standing in line at the local multiplex cinema.

As I have observed my own life as a gay man and the lives of many of my gay clients, there is a curious and consistent theme that emerges. Regardless of how successful or wealthy we may or may not be, we are almost always over-the-top outrageous in what we do. We are the chefs at the best, most highly reviewed restaurants. We are the vice presidents of important investment houses. We are the top hairstylists to whom movie stars fly for hundreds of miles just to have us fix their hair. We rarely do things that are quiet, reserved, and commonplace. Those jobs we leave by and large to straight people to slog through.

There is a definite *outrageous* quality to our lives. Years ago, when I first took notice of this, I began asking myself "Why?" What is it about loving another man that leads us to be outrageous? The two, in my mind, seemed completely unrelated, and yet they seemed to be very common partners in real life. Gay and outrageous. Yes, that more or less described many of the gay men I knew.

Not until I began the deeper work of uncovering shame in my own life and the lives of my gay clients did I understand this connection. Let me start to explain

> "I never owned a tuxedo until I moved to San Francisco. I have never been invited to so many black tie events. When the invitation arrives in the mail, you know it's one more lavish party that is trying to outdo the one before."
>
> STEVE FROM SAN FRANCISCO, CA

this by asking a question: If you hold the fundamental assumption of shame that you are critically and mortally flawed, how would you cope with this? One way, as we have seen in stage one, is to avoid confronting the shame. Another way, the way of so many of us, is to compensate for shame by striving for validation from others, even if it is not earned authentically. As long as others are actively acknowledging our superior and creative accomplishments, we can at least temporarily convince ourselves that we aren't so bad after all. If everyone else thinks we're great, are we not great?

Stage two of the gay man's life is the stage of compensating for shame. Once we leave stage one and are no longer shamed by our sexuality, we continue to hold the deeper belief that there is something fundamentally flawed about ourselves. Any person, straight or gay, who grows up in an environment that is essentially invalidating of some core part of themselves such as sexuality struggles with this deeper shame. The shame over being gay is past us. Now we are driven by the deeper shame of believing that we are flawed.

While we grow ever more comfortable with our sexuality, in both public and private, we have yet to deal with the core shame that continues to hound us. We grew up believing that we were unacceptable and somehow tragically twisted. We no longer hold that being gay is twisted, but we cling to the core belief that we are inferior.

In stage two, it is this core of toxic shame that takes center stage. To silence the distress of this toxic shame, we go about the task of seeking validation from others. However we can and with whatever abilities we are blessed with, we set about to mine the world for approval, praise, and recognition. The more validation we discover, the less distress we feel.

What's different about our craving for validation in stage two is that in stage one, validation is all about trying to hide our sexuality. In stage two, it is about trying to still the small but persistent voice of shame within us. We need validation to assure us that as gay men, we are worthwhile and ultimately deserving of love.

The acquisition of validation is so rewarding that we become validation junkies. The more we get, the more we crave it, the better we feel, and the harder it becomes for us to tolerate invalidation. Our houses become showplaces that elicit kudos from all who enter. Our bodies become chiseled in muscle, pleasing our bedroom guests. We work to become wealthy so that we can take regular and exotic excursions around the world that bring us excitement and worldly sophistication that is recognized and adored by other wealthy, worldly travelers. We write books, create the world's most recognized art, and collect everything from stamps to the finest pedigree bulldogs. Explore the finest of anything in this world and you will always find gay men clustered about the helm.

And, of course, we include sex in our search for validation. Many gay men collect encounters with beautiful, sexy men like a museum might hoard all the David Hockney or Edward Hopper paintings it can possibly afford.

The validation we achieve through sexual encounters is immediate and stimulating, even if it is essentially inauthentic. We play a role, one that we have mastered over years of being onstage, that seduces our beautiful conquest-to-be. When he gives up his resistance and succumbs to our siren call, we feel the rush of immediate validation. If no one else does, at least this one man sees something of value in us. This blissful moment rarely lingers, but in that moment, it satisfies.

Hidden in our search for validation is both a truth and a lie. The truth is that validation is good and necessary for our psychological well-being. The lie is that we have not yet truly discovered or accepted ourselves; hence, the validation is of something less than authentic. It is the validation of a façade that we masterfully erect.

In fact, in our rush to achieve validation, we run roughshod over the subtleties that lie within us, and choose instead to grab the nearest and brightest flag that will draw the attention and, hopefully, validation of the world around us. In stage two, we learn to achieve validation in any way that we can, and not necessarily in the ways that will make us content with life.

During stage two, more so than any other stage, a low tolerance for invalidation rises to the surface. This is an inability to tolerate any perceived invalidation that might come our way.

Sometimes it is painful invalidation, like a lover who leaves you for another man or a friend who stabs you in the back with critical words spoken to others. Sometimes it is a slight invalidation, perhaps just a frown from a stranger or an innocent joke about your taste in clothing. Whatever the source and however intense the perceived invalidation, in stage two, the gay man can handle very little of it.

A friend of mine who happens to be a medical doctor relayed to me a good example of this inability to tolerate invalidation that he experienced in a relationship with a friend. He had scheduled a lunch with a gay friend, John. The two of them had met when they were in high school and had remained close for almost twenty years. In the past few years, they didn't see each other as often as they'd like given my friend's busy schedule of seeing patients and making hospital rounds. Right before the time of their lunch, my friend received an urgent page from the hospital about a patient who was dying from a mistake one of the nurses had made in administering medication. My friend raced to the hospital, and as soon as he could, called John to apologize and to see if they could reschedule the lunch. John was cool on the phone and agreed to meet at some future date. After that, my friend didn't hear from John for weeks, even though he left several messages on his answering machine. When they finally did speak some months after the lunch incident, John was irate with my friend and accused him of never caring enough and having been a terrible friend. He angrily declared that the friendship was now over.

My friend was truly devastated over the incident. He felt bad about having had to cancel the lunch, but at the same time he knew that he had no other choice. No matter how much he tried to explain this to John, it didn't seem to matter. John had perceived the incident as deeply invalidating and was clearly very angry about it.

Perhaps in reading this example you may feel that John was unusually childish and rash in his response. And he was. But take a moment and consider that if you have known other gay men in stage two, then you have had similar experiences. You may even be able to recall times when you reacted just as John did. I'm certainly not proud of it, but I must admit that I can.

When a gay man experiences a low tolerance for invalidation, he is highly distressed by whatever perceived invalidation he experiences, and it is only logical that he would take action to relieve that distress. That action, or shall I call it a reaction, usually involves either removing himself from the invalidating situation, silencing the source of invalidation, or both.

> "My last boyfriend was so sensitive that he'd walk out of the house just because he thought I gave him a dirty look. Even when I was trying to be loving and understanding, he'd find some way that I was being critical or mean. Living with him was like walking on thin ice ... you never knew when it would break and you'd plunge into freezing cold water."
>
> ANTONIO FROM ATLANTA, GA

In practical terms, this means that we either avoid the person who is invalidating us or we strike out at them verbally, physically, or passively. In the case of John, he verbally attacked my friend and then avoided potential future invalidation by terminating the friendship.

There are many ways a gay man in stage two might react to invalidation. If he is in a position of power, he may fire the employee on the spot who invalidates his decision-making abilities. Or he may walk off the job when the boss points out a problem in his work. He may verbally shred a neighbor who objects to the addition he is planning for his house.

These, of course, are very active and obvious ways the gay man in stage two may react to invalidation. As mentioned earlier, however, there are also more passive means. He may not be able to afford to walk off the job when a coworker criticizes his work, but for months afterward he simply refuses to be helpful in any way or sabotages the coworker's project by acting as if he never received the memo asking him for assistance. He may emotionally shut down with his lover after a perceived invalidation and refuse to share anything other than the mundane details of life for some time following the incident.

Without a doubt, sex is a major source of invalidation within relationships between gay men. When one partner refuses the other partner's bid for sex, it can start a chain of sexual withholding that has destroyed more than few gay male relationships. The rejected partner perceives a deep and intolerable invalidation by being turned down, and he reacts by withdrawing sexually. The other partner, invalidated by this, equally withdraws and the sexual aspect of the relationship goes stale.

Therapists who work with gay male couples often report seeing this cycle of "mutual invalidation" in their clients' relationships. I remember working with a gay couple a few years ago who had reached the brink of disaster. Both men came to therapy on the verge of leaving, so much so that at the time I was surprised that they even bothered to seek help. The more I probed in the first session, the more it became clear that these two had been through years of active invalidation of one another.

When the couple returned after that very tedious and painful first session, I learned of even more pain that plagued these two men. At some point, one of them had an affair with a close friend of theirs. The other one found out about the affair and started blatantly soliciting men in one of the local gay bars for sex, right in front of his partner. And things got worse. He started bringing men to the house and having sex with them at times when he knew his partner could easily come home. For a short time, the other partner moved in with the friend with whom he was having the affair. This torturous game had gone on for years, back and forth, and it had destroyed virtually every ounce of good feeling between them.

While no gay man is proud of it, it is true that gay men in stage two can become absolute geniuses at invalidating each other. Because we have such a low tolerance for invalidation and experience it so painfully, we also are hypersensitive to it in our environment. In other words, we're always on the lookout for invalidation. As a result, we come to know it in all its forms and nuance. So when the time comes that we need to strike back at a perceived invalidation, what might we deliver? A good smack of the same in return.

The stereotype of the bitchy, bitter queen comes from the image of the gay man who is stuck in stage two. He knows to expect invalidation, and he is armed with fistfuls of it in return. "Don't mess with me, sister, cause I'll bite back and bite back hard."

Depression can emerge in the gay man in stage two as it can in stage one, but for different reasons. In stage two, the gay man experiences a hunger for validation and a hypersensitivity to invalidation. In fact, he may become so sensitized to invalidation that he begins to see it everywhere he turns in life. His vision narrows, as if by intention he were eliminating from sight all traces of validation. What he does allow himself to see is a life full of invalidation.

A colleague of mine recently treated a twenty-eight-year-old gay man who worked at a high-tech company in California. The man had come to therapy on the verge of suicide. As the therapist worked with him, the source of his hopeless depression began to emerge: he was a failure. Because he hadn't chosen to work for a firm where his stock options would now be worth millions of dollars, his current paycheck of $250,000 per year gravely reminded him that he was a failure.

"Wow!" you might say. "That's screwed up." And it is—on a very grand scale. But the dynamic underlying this incredible misperception of reality is common among gay men experiencing depression in stage two. Everything starts to sour and go bad—even the good things in life. It's as if everything has become infected with invalidation. And the experience is deeply distressing and hopeless.

While not all gay men in the throes of stage two experience this depression, a sizable number do. The toxic core of shame has the gay man utterly convinced that he is critically flawed, and this shame colors and dims his experience of life, causing him to filter out the good and grasp only the bad, difficult, and distressing.

What is distinctly noticeable about this stage two depression is that the old sources of validation no longer seem to soothe the gay man's distress. He works hard, but the feeling of validation is harder to come by. The beautifully furnished apartment no longer thrills him. His success at work feels as if it were a grating noise to his ears. The parade of sexual conquests with beautiful men becomes tedious and boring, like a hamster on a treadmill who runs incessantly but will never go anywhere. Very little, if anything, is experienced as validating.

The resolution of this depression is the same thing that takes all gay men from stage two to stage three. In short, he must discover the secret of *authentic* validation.

The primary thrust of stage two is achieving validation as compensation for shame. Along with this naturally follows a very low tolerance for invalidation. Stage two is a race against shame—pushing as hard as we can to earn the prize that will make it all worthwhile. The problem arises, however, in that not all validation really satisfies us. Some forms of validation, the more inauthentic forms, briefly gratify our hunger but ultimately only whet our appetite for more. In the end, it is only authentic validation that truly satisfies us, and when we are starved for authentic validation, depression inevitably overtakes us.

The harsh reality of stage two is that the gay man often pursues sources of inauthentic validation. Why? Because he hasn't yet discovered the essential part of himself. Having lived with the belief that he was critically flawed, his true self was abandoned and he pursued other, more appealing personas.

The steep climb out of stage two and the depression it can sometimes trigger is found in the simple process of rediscovering the essence of the self. It is a complete upheaval of life that ultimately destroys everything that was once dear and sacred, and preserves only that which is real and honest.

In order to discover the self, we must first face our core of shame. We must acknowledge that we have long held a belief in our own reprehension, and this belief has directed our life, and not for the better. Perhaps this seems the obvious and logical path as we objectively consider shame, but the subjective experience of facing toxic shame is utterly wrenching. It quakes even the most stable part of our soul, and leaves us terrified by the knowledge that we know nothing of who we truly are.

This exposure to toxic shame causes it to erode and melt, eventually leaving us for good. Like fear or any other distressing emotion, prolonged exposure diminishes its power over us. When we stand and face that wicked witch, she dissolves under the power of our steadfast gaze.

The end of stage two is inevitably the dark night of the soul for the gay man. It is a time when he may untie every anchor to his small vessel. Relationships are often ended. Career choices are frequently questioned. Friendships are dismissed. The meaning of life is rejected, revised, destroyed, and reinvented. And while the extent to which a gay man displays this angst upon his face and life may vary, the internal process is always tough and grim. Some retreat into a period of mostly silent contemplation. Others become activated, expressing their struggle to all who will hear. Each slight variation of personality has its own way of expressing the process, but the result is the same: elimination of shame and the birth of authenticity.

Chapter 8

STUCK IN SHAME:
THE VICIOUS CYCLE

The first two stages of the gay man's emotional life contain within them a troubling and self-defeating cycle that is often difficult to break. In fact, it is this vicious cycle that keeps some gay men locked into stages one and two for a lifetime.

The vicious cycle is an inability to learn from one's mistakes in life as a result of avoiding shame. Mistakes are one of the primary causes of justifiable shame. Therefore, when a gay man in stage one or two makes a mistake, he is slow to admit it and stubbornly refuses to revisit the mistake in order to learn how he might do things better. He may employ defensive behaviors such as blaming the mistake on others, denial, and being slow or refusing to acknowledge the mistake.

Randy had been frustrated with his job for several months. He had quickly shimmied up the management hierarchy at his company over the past few years, and now found himself in an administrative position that had almost nothing to do with the work he really enjoyed. He had been a graphic designer for an advertising firm, and when he showed some talent for managing projects, he soon found himself being promoted into a management position. On top of this, his new boss was extremely hard-driving and difficult to work for. One day late in November, he went to work and discovered one of his boss's usual demanding voicemails waiting for him. (His boss had a habit of not sleeping and sending voicemails to employees in the middle of the night.) It was just too much for Randy, and he walked into his boss's office and quit.

The months that followed his resignation were very lean, to say the least. The rent in San Francisco wasn't cheap, and he chewed through the little bit in savings he had in a matter of weeks. He couldn't claim unemployment benefits because he had voluntarily quit his job, and his field was not hiring. He ended up losing his apartment, moving in with a friend, running up his credit cards to the limit, and working a part-time job at a local real estate firm laying out their Sunday advertisements.

Because the whole situation triggered a great deal of shame for Randy, he couldn't see that he had made a mistake by quitting without having another job lined up. He blamed his old boss, the slow economy, and his "greedy" landlord for his current problems.

Had Randy been able to tolerate the shame over having reacted too quickly, he could have then been able to acknowledge that he sometimes acted impulsively, not usually in his best interest. The next time such a situation would come up, he'd be able to recognize the signs of impulsivity and attempt to work things out in a more thoughtful and planned manner. But Randy just couldn't go there—the shame was too much for him. Not surprisingly, he repeated similar scenarios in several subsequent jobs.

Like with Randy, a common experience of gay men in stages one and two is this difficulty in learning from past mistakes. Mistakes trigger shame; therefore, they must be avoided. Since no one is perfect, mistakes are unavoidable, so the second-best thing he can do is avoid the memory of the mistakes, or try to "cook the books" and construe the mistake as something other than an error. The tragedy contained in this vicious cycle is that mistakes help a person change their behavior. When mistakes are swept under the carpet of life, then no change takes place and the same dysfunctional behaviors keep happening.

One area in stages one and two where the vicious cycle is quite evident is when a gay man jumps from one relationship to another, seemingly without much hesitation in between. Because the shame over a failed relationship is too distressing, he chooses to fill his mind with other things rather than rethinking the memory of the failed relationship. Of course, there's no better distraction in life than to fall head over heels for another man. By throwing himself into another relationship quickly, there is little time or energy to mull over the problems of the past. When memories do surface, he often handles them by blaming them on the shortcomings of his former partner. The more he pushes the memories away, the more effectively he avoids shame.

> "Ten years later when I went back to the gay neighborhood where I had lived for years, I was really surprised to find many of the same men doing the same things . . . going to the bars, picking up a guy, and rushing home to have sex. I couldn't help but wonder, 'Why haven't they moved on in life?'"
>
> CLYDE FROM SONOMA COUNTY, CA

There are brief times when the gay man cannot deny the mistakes of his past. Quite unpredictably the memories can come boiling to the surface, and he may find himself overwhelmed and even incapacitated. This is the time when most gay men in stages one and two seek psychotherapy. For a brief window, they see a glimpse of themselves clearly, and it triggers such overwhelming and toxic shame that they have great difficulty functioning normally.

Psychotherapy with a gay man in such a crisis is often difficult for the therapist. The therapist may want him to examine and learn from the mistakes of his past, but this only increases his distress and feelings of shame. Instead, what the client seeks is support for his defensive behaviors. He wants the therapist to collude with him in blaming his ex-partners, ex-bosses, or former friends. If the therapist is unwilling to do so, the client may become angry toward the therapist and be unwilling to continue. What he seeks is help in avoiding shame, not more exposure to shame. It's not until he reaches stage three that he realizes that the only way to reduce shame is to expose oneself to it. Until he's ready, he will likely resist any attempt that comes close to increasing his experience of shame.

> "There were times when I would wake up in the night distraught by the feeling that I had been the worst friend and lover ever. I can't explain it, but suddenly every deceptive, secretive deed came flooding back to me and it felt horrible."
>
> JOHN FROM ALBUQUERQUE, NM

Being unable to acknowledge mistakes of the past is often a challenge in intimate relationships. Every relationship requires repair from time to time—one or both people must own the injury they have caused within the relationship and show an intention to do differently in the future. Nobody wants to be around a jerk who never acknowledges when he has screwed up. Eventually, we grow weary of such a person and break off the relationship.

Admitting a mistake is opening the door to shame, something a gay man in stages one and two can't really afford to do. It's far too threatening, so he may ignore the mistake and hope it will be forgotten, or worse, try to create a distraction by blaming his partner for something else.

Geoff and Randy were always arguing about something. It seemed that every day brought some new dispute, however minor, that sparked at a minimum an enlivened discussion. Whether to buy soy or rice milk, when to have the dog groomed, how best to clean the kitchen—on and on it went.

When they came in for couple's counseling, they both complained that the other couldn't ever apologize for his mistakes. This would then inspire the other to refuse to apologize or offer a repair, and so the relationship polarized between two men who were unwilling to own the injuries each may have created in the relationship.

What Geoff and Randy experienced had begun to tear their relationship apart. Privately, each felt responsible for the failure of the relationship, but when they were together neither was willing to do so, at least not in a meaningful way. For example, when Geoff would apologize for something he'd done, he'd inevitably follow it with reciprocal blame of Randy, effectively undoing the apology. "It's true that I didn't take the dog out last night, but it was only because Randy didn't do the dishes and I was busy cleaning up after him." Repairing a relationship means taking meaningful steps to accept responsibility without diverting to blame for another issue. By offering a counter-blame, Geoff was able to stave off the shame by showing that in comparison his mistakes were somehow less than Randy's.

I see often the tactic of counter-blame in gay couples where both men are in stage one or two. Even in relationships that are far less conflicted than Geoff and Randy's, you see it come out whenever the subject turns to important problems within the relationship. "I would want to have more sex if he were interested in kissing more." Or "I only went out to the bar because he doesn't seem to be interested in me anymore." These and so many other situations are fraught with possibilities for counter-blame.

Another common experience with these couples is that of pseudo-apologies. Because owning a mistake is shame-provoking only when you really believe that you are responsible, it is possible to apologize for a long list of things that you really don't believe you have done but will earn you points with your partner. Unfortunately, pseudo-apologies contribute to a reserve of resentment that continues to grow within you. You slowly trade some of your self-esteem for the sake of diffusing a possible conflict. You begin to feel like the martyr as the resentment mounts—the one who is always making sacrifices for the sake of the relationship.

How does this play out? One way is when gay men become completely infatuated and obsessed with a new love. It is beyond enjoying the excitement of a new man in their life—they become consumed with the relationship, spending virtually all of their time with the new lover and neglecting their relationships with just about anyone else. As the relationship begins to cool down, they begin to notice small faults in their lover and begin pointing these out. Eventually, this creates an explosive situation, as the criticism sparks shame and anger within the lover, and he may choose to retaliate with some choice criticisms of his own. The relationship often continues for a while—sometimes months or even years—with both partners constantly needling and triggering shame in each other. At some point, it becomes too much and the relationship falls apart.

Amazingly, for some gay men this cycle may mature in only a couple of weeks, and for others it may take significantly longer.

One day he is on cloud nine with a new love. Before you know it, he despises the same man. I once knew a gay man who told his friend, "Don't even bother to introduce me until you've been with him (new boyfriend) for six months. I don't want to waste time with the flavor-of-the-month man."

A gay man who spends a great deal of time spinning around and around in this vicious cycle inevitably experiences a relationship trauma. Betrayal, abandonment, abuse, and chaotic relationships are all part of his history. He may even develop relationship hopelessness and decide that this is all relationships will ever be for him. And this being so, he concludes that they are just too much work for him.

What eventually breaks this vicious cycle? It is the slow process of learning to tolerate and reduce shame rather than avoid it. He can learn from the mistakes of his past only if he is willing to carefully examine them. When these mistakes remain shrouded in shame, he cannot afford to investigate his own life. He keeps moving forward, trying not to look back, and as a result, finds himself going in a circle. When he learns skills for dealing with shame, he eventually realizes that he can tolerate the distress of examining his past. With the shame reduced, he can begin the work of clearly seeing his own behavior patterns and making needed changes.

Chapter 9

IN THE MOOD
FOR A MAN

Kyle passed the same public park on his way to work every day. Often he would take note of the cars in the park's lot. There was rarely anyone in view; the owners of those cars were traversing the wooded trails just on the other side of the lot. The trails really didn't go anywhere, but of course, that wasn't the point. These were "sex trails" and the park was at times one of the busiest places in town to hook up with other gay men.

At least twice a week, Kyle would leave a half hour earlier than he needed to for work, just so he could stop by the park and check out the scene. If someone caught his eye, he would follow him into the woods until they both found a place that felt safely camouflaged. There they would grope each other, perhaps jerk off, or have oral sex. He'd be back in his car in no less than twenty minutes and on his way to work.

Kyle hated his job. He held the title of program director at a nonprofit organization, but the reality was that he was little more than a secretary for the executive director. Every chance he could during the day, he would log on to a porno website and spend a few minutes surfing its content. Mostly, Kyle was excruciatingly bored and somewhat depressed about the state of his career.

Kyle was very clear about why he stopped by the park so often. It was without a doubt the only excitement in his day. It was the one thing he looked forward to and the suspense over who he might meet enlivened him. The park made him forget about his dead-end job, even if it was for just a few precious minutes.

Some gay men in stages one and two use sex as Kyle did: to help manage their emotions. Whenever they start to feel lonely, sad, anxious, or bored, they head to the local gay bar, bathhouse, park, rest stop, chat room . . . you name it, to meet up for quick, anonymous sex. The distraction the sex provides helps them to break the ongoing flow of whatever distressing emotion they are currently feeling. When it's over with, the distress may return, but often it is somewhat reduced.

> "There have been many days where the only thing that kept me from walking off this wretched job was knowing that I might pick up someone new that evening. You never know who you'll meet: sometimes it's an old troll and sometimes Bingo!—you win the gay lottery! If it weren't for that adrenaline rush, life would be pretty dull."
>
> JESSE FROM MIAMI, FL

The real detriment in such behavior—aside from such dangers as HIV and the destruction of committed relationships—lies in the fact that sex with men becomes a necessary method for changing your mood or alleviating distress. It begins to play a central role in your psychological equilibrium, and you can't effectively function without it. Whenever things get rough at work or home, you head for the nearest place to hook up with men.

This is what is known as a *process addiction*—using a behavior to regulate your mood. At first, any process addiction is a choice

to engage in a behavior that helps to radically shift your mood.
Over time, you become dependent on the behavior, and it starts to
feel like it's out of control. Regardless of the consequences of re-
peating this behavior, you keep doing it to feel better. Again and
again, you go do it, until you either find another way to regulate
your life becomes
consumed with the addiction.

"I'll never forget my visit to Fire Is-
land. There was more sex happening between the dunes on the
beach than I'd ever seen. There
were groups of men everywhere
doing it right on the beach."

DWIGHT FROM NEW YORK, NY

Gay men who actively participate in frequent anonymous or
casual sexual hookups are loath
to call what they are doing an addiction, but the signs are all there.
If you look just beneath the surface, you find a life that is con-
sumed with pursuing sex. They *need* the sex to make life livable,
and in the process, often destroy the best things in their life. Relationship after relationship falls apart because they either have
an affair or become so miserable when the relationship cools off
sexually that they feel compelled to find a new supplier of the
drug they crave, walking away from lover after lover to find it.

So, exactly how do gay men use sex to manage their moods?
To start, let's take an emotion, such as loneliness or anxiety, that
causes you to panic and begin to think all kinds of catastrophic
thoughts. "I'll always be lonely, and eventually die a lonely old
man." Or "I'm completely incapable, and I can't handle this."
Each emotion has its own set of common catastrophic thoughts
that it can trigger, but the result is the same. Not only do you feel
the distressing emotion, you panic because it feels as if the emotion will never pass. The emotion becomes intolerable, and you
search in earnest for a way to avoid feeling it. That's where brief
sexual encounters often enter the picture—not only do they

bring distraction, they sometimes hold the power to change your mood completely.

Of all the distressing emotions that can induce the gay man to seek out sex, loneliness is probably top on the list. Loneliness as an emotion has some unique properties, and the foremost is that the more a gay man tries to avoid confronting his loneliness, the more control the emotion has over his life. The fear of being lonely increases, and the anticipated distress heightens dramatically. It's like the monster under the bed: The longer you are unwilling to look under the bed, the greater your fear grows. Not until one of your parents forced you to look under the bed and see that there was no monster hiding there did the fear begin to decrease. Likewise, not until you are willing to sit with your feelings of loneliness are you able to realize that it really isn't all that distressing, and most of the time, passes quickly.

> "When it comes down to it, isn't having a boyfriend, however brief, better than none at all? Is that pathetic?"
>
> TOMAS FROM CINCINNATI, OH

Instead of allowing himself to feel lonely, the gay man may try to avoid it by seeking out a brief sexual encounter. As long as he is engaged in the "chase" and eventually captures his prize, he is emotionally distracted and his mood often shifts. The problem is, however, that this effect is usually temporary, and often the loneliness (or threat of loneliness) returns. The gay man must do it all over again.

Learning to effectively manage your emotions is a skill that is often underrated in its importance. Each of us feels many different emotions during the day, from joy and happiness to anger and sadness. Being able to manage those feelings effectively and prevent yourself from being overwhelmed by them is a key to fulfillment and, in most areas of life, success.

Kyle relied heavily on sex to regulate his emotions. This worked for him until the day that he got into a relationship with a really wonderful man. It was only a matter of time before the relationship sparked some distress, and Kyle started feeling the strong urge to seek out sex with other men. In his more rational state of mind, he didn't want to do anything to hurt his relationship, but when he was distressed with emotion, all he wanted to do was escape into the embrace of another man. As a few years passed, Kyle secretly returned to his habit of frequenting the park. Now he was feeling terrible guilt about his behavior and wanting to change before his lover found out about what he had been doing.

John and Joe had been in a relationship for many years. John consistently wanted sex more than Joe, although Joe felt that he had a perfectly healthy sexual appetite. John, on the other hand, became noticeably upset whenever they went more than a few days without having sex. Joe complained that when they had sex, it often felt mechanical and thoughtless. He described it as a "compulsion" of John's that he was expected to comply with on a regular basis.

Like in the case of John and Joe, more than a few gay couples have the problem of one partner wanting sex more often than the other partner. Of course, this is not always because the over-sexed partner is using sex as a way to regulate his emotions, but often it is, particularly when the lack of sex creates inordinate distress for the partner. It takes on a great importance in the relationship, and can become a serious problem that drives two men apart.

Some gay men who have a particularly difficult time with self-validation rely on sex to feel good about themselves. This kind of gay man needs to see others excited by his presence and adoring his body in order to feel worthwhile and acceptable. If other gay men fail to notice him or be attracted to him, he begins to question his own value. On the surface, this may sound a bit juvenile, but in reality it is something that many, if not most, gay men struggle with to some degree. We rely heavily upon the adoring reactions of others to our presence for our own self-esteem.

ETERNALLY SEXY

When a gay man relies on sex for his self-esteem, he often develops something of a phobia about aging. Age, in his mind, becomes synonymous with "no sex," and he decides that he'd rather be dead than to become an old man. There is some interesting research that shows a sizeable minority of gay men engage in unprotected, high-risk sexual acts because they'd rather die young than grow old.

Thinking back on my twenties when I lived in San Francisco, I remember walking past the Twin Peaks, a gay bar with huge glass windows that face both Castro and Market Streets. Inside, I'd always notice the older clientele who sat at the bar, drinking the afternoon away. "Wrinkle room" we'd call it as we walked by, hoping upon hope that we would never become that old and alone.

The obsession with looking younger, even when you're clearly not, can be seen in almost any gay neighborhood. A close observer will notice everything from dye jobs to cover up the gray, face lifts to remove the wrinkles, liposuction for the love handles, and chest implants for a more muscled look. Younger means we are more attractive, and being more attractive means we will still be sexually viable.

There's nothing wrong in wanting to look younger, but when it takes on such an importance in our lives that we are willing to do just about anything to hang on to the illusion of youth, it is symptomatic of a deeper issue. We don't have meaning in our lives without sex. There is no joy in our lives without sex.

The gay man's obsession with youth is almost always linked with his use of sex as a way to control his emotions. He imagines that when he is no longer sexually attractive, he will become overwhelmed by his loneliness and a victim to depression. There will be no way to bring joy into his life anymore. Life will become drudgery and painful.

What he doesn't realize is that gay men who no longer use sex to control their emotions are often relieved to grow older. The pressure to be sexy and out on the town is lifted. He no longer feels compelled to watch every calorie that passes his lips or spend seven hours a week at the gym. Instead, he is free to be himself, without all the cultural expectations that he be something else or that he must, at all costs, remain alluring to other men.

> "I never thought I'd live to be fifty. I used to think, 'Who wants an old man?' I really believed it would be better to be dead than grow old, fat, and wrinkled."
>
> JOHN FROM ALBUQUERQUE, NM

Using other men as a method of emotion regulation requires the gay man to be fundamentally inauthentic. The sexual encounter is all about making him feel something different, and when that is successfully accomplished, he is done with the other man. The encounter is a means to an end that has little to do with a relationship or emotional exchange between two people. It's all about me and making me feel better, and you are forced to go through the motions, pretending to be interested in the other person long enough to get him naked. At times, you must make idle conversation until sufficient time has passed so that both of you can maintain the illusion that it really isn't just about sex. For instance, you may learn that at times it is more effective toward your goal of having sex if you aren't exactly honest about all the details of your life. You may be even tempted to create a completely fabricated life just for the benefit of bedding the listener (if you have any doubt about this, just visit a gay chat room on the internet).

The authenticity that is sought in stage three is fundamentally inconsistent with the use of sex as an emotion regulation method. In stage three, the gay man must learn other ways than just sex to control his emotions, improve his mood, and to find joy in life.

Sex is not the only process addiction that gay men pursue. For example, some pursue pornography and XXX internet sites. Others use gambling, food, or shopping to regulate their mood.

Sergio is a well-known designer in his mid-sixties. He and his lover of twenty-five years live in a beautifully decorated apartment in San Francisco overlooking the bay and the Golden Gate Bridge. From the outside, Sergio looks as if he is the model of success, and in many ways, he is. What isn't quite so apparent is that Sergio usually does not have more than a few hundred dollars to his name. He's created a fabulous illusion of wealth by living in an apartment owned by an adoring client who rents to him and his lover for next to nothing. The exquisite furnishings were mostly purchased as add-ons and kickbacks from shop owners who appreciated Sergio directing his clients to their shops, so they passed on a few gifts for him under the table.

The truth is, Sergio makes a great living. The other, hidden truth is that he spends everything he makes and then some shopping. He buys only the best-quality and finest collectibles. At every store in San Francisco and New York he has huge charge accounts and items on layaway. He shops and shops and shops. And the more stressed he becomes, the more he shops.

Sergio's lover is also in his mid-sixties, but neither Sergio nor his lover will be able to retire soon—or perhaps ever. The truth is that Sergio even convinced his lover to cash in his retirement account to fund the purchase of extremely rare antique rugs that he "just had to have."

Sergio is addicted to shopping. Whenever he needs to change his mood, he shops. While he doesn't acknowledge his shopping as a problem, it doesn't take much analysis to see that he and his lover have paid a high price for his addiction. After years of such behavior, their lives are driven by the need to buy and pay for what Sergio has already purchased. They have become slaves to his endless hunger to shop.

Not every gay man in stages one and two develops a process addiction, but more than a few do. Ultimately, these additions are a small, leaky lifeboat in the high tide of shame. They protect, if only for the moment, the gay man from drowning in the shame that threatens to consume his life and soul. The gay man who floats in this tide must have his lifeboat to survive. Without it, life truly isn't worth living.

If you've had a process addiction or known someone close who has, imagine this: At the height of the addiction, would life be worth living if you couldn't have sex? Couldn't party? Couldn't get high? Couldn't shop?

As with any true addiction, life is unimaginable without it. Hopelessness and shame begin to rise higher and higher, and the addict secretly wonders if it's worth going on without the addiction.

Not until the gay man develops another way to manage his emotions can he leave his addictions behind. When he learns how to authentically connect with his world and achieve the contentment that he craves, he can relinquish those old behaviors and break free from their suffocation. Here lies the boundary between stages two and three. The gay man begins to leave behind the inauthenticity of his past, and moves into a place of becoming himself—a true self that is shown to all the world for the flawed beauty therein. But first, he must pass through another ring of fire: the crisis of meaning.

Chapter 10

WHAT'S IT ALL ABOUT?

A CRISIS OF MEANING

Stage two culminates in a desperate search for meaning in life. Are "white" parties and beautiful men, elegant houses, and chic dinner parties really all there is to life? Years of compensating for shame in a myriad of ways brings him to his knees, exhausted and confused. The one thing he had fought so hard to earn—acceptance of his sexuality—has led him into a life that has been difficult, often lonely, and far less fulfilling than he had imagined.

When Jerome finally accepted his sexuality, he left the priesthood. Not that he was forced out, but he left of his own desire for freedom to really discover who he was. He had been a respected diocesan Catholic priest since his early twenties, and before that he had always been committed to becoming a priest. Now in his mid-thirties, he was questioning all of those commitments. Yes, he was gay, and he began to wonder if he entered the priesthood only to hide his sexuality.

After almost ten years of life post-priesthood, Jerome found himself struggling with the real meaning of life. Although he left the priesthood, he had never truly left the faith that had been his since childhood. He had walked away from his vocation and burned a few bridges in the leaving. Now he was looking back and wondering if it was the right decision.

Jerome's crisis of meaning reached a peak, and attempting to resolve it, he approached the archbishop about returning to active ministry. Nothing he had done as an "out" gay man had given him contentment, and now he was looking back at the priesthood wondering if he hadn't given up the one thing that held real promise for him. Maybe it had been a mistake to leave.

> "Peggy Lee got it right when she sang, 'Is That All There Is?' By the time I was forty-five, I felt I had seen and done it all. Now what?"
>
> DOUG FROM LOS ANGELES, CA

Jerome wasn't questioning his sexuality. He knew he was gay through and through. He had had a few lovers and many sexual partners during his break from the ministry and had thoroughly explored his sexual appetites. While it had been great fun at times and satisfied a burning curiosity within him, it didn't give him the contented feeling that he had imagined it would. Perhaps he could live as a gay man and return to the one sure calling he had felt in life.

Gay men in their forties and fifties often enter the crisis of meaning. What's happiness really all about? How will I find lasting love and contentment? Can I find it in a relationship with a man? Is there such a thing as a healthy relationship between two men? How can I find real purpose and passion in my life?

Like the crisis of identity, the crisis of meaning can either be foreclosed or resolved. Foreclosure is what it always is—nothing more than a quick fix to a distressing emotional state. In the crisis of meaning, it usually means throwing yourself into another relationship, buying yet another vacation home, traveling around the world, or pushing yourself to create the perfect body. Foreclosure in the crisis of meaning almost always sounds something like this: "I'll find contentment if I just try harder at what I've been doing." More men. More sex. More workouts. More parties. More high achievement. More money. More Botox. More, bigger, better.

Chris's partner died five years ago from a quick but acute case of hepatitis C. Chris was left grieving, with a house that was midway in an extensive remodeling job, and in a city where he hadn't really wanted to live. For the past fifteen years, Chris had built his life primarily around his partner's life. Now he was alone with a life he didn't want.

A year and a half went by and Chris finished the house and sold it. In fact, he sold everything except a few small pieces of furniture, a car, and his clothes. He took the money and went on an around-the-world trip. That, he imagined, would give some direction in his life.

On a three-week stop in Australia, he met a fine young man who was ten years his junior. He was a handsome guy, to say the least, and loved to party. Soon, he and Chris were out at the clubs nightly until dawn. The excitement of new love and reinvigorated libido gave Chris the hope that he had found what he was looking for.

Six months later, Chris returned to the apartment in Sydney that he had bought a month after meeting his new boyfriend to find that he wasn't the only man his boyfriend was sleeping with. He packed a few bags, and less than a week later was back in the United States, not really sure where he was ultimately headed. Maybe L.A.? Maybe Palm Springs? Maybe New York City?

Chris bounced around from boyfriend to boyfriend for a few years, growing more depressed and cynical. Men were dogs, and he was hopelessly attracted to them. He'd swear off men for good, only to find himself back at the kennel looking for another one to relieve his grinding boredom with life.

Chris foreclosed on his crisis of meaning time and again. As far as I know, he still hasn't resolved it. Last I heard, he was living in Palm Springs and working as a real estate agent.

Resolving the crisis of meaning is all about reaching the place of honest and radical authenticity. It's about no longer needing to compensate for shame and living your life without needing to gild it with the extraordinary. Growing older, day by day and year by year, without the need to make it all seem better than it really is. It's life, and it's just fine without the embellishments.

The one and only skill that resolves the crisis of meaning is that of acceptance. Learning to accept the things in life as they are in the present moment. You're growing older, your boyfriend's getting fatter, your job isn't totally amazing, and where you live can often be boring. To repeat a cliché that I often breathe to myself: "It is what it is."

When you drop the struggle with shame and accept life as it is without judgment, you find great freedom on the other side. It is freedom to be who you are, exactly as you are. The only real meaning in life is found in being who you are right now, without apologies.

You don't need to be more spiritual, richer, friendlier, better looking, younger, or living on a beach. In this moment, all you need to be is you. Only in that space will you find lasting contentment.

The journey into authenticity and acceptance is the beginning of stage three in the gay man's life. It is the final stage in life, no matter at what age it is entered. Stage three is the final good-bye to toxic shame and the beginning of a life that is truly worth living.

STAGE 3: CULTIVATING AUTHENTICITY

"We have a hunger for something like authenticity, but are easily satisfied by an ersatz facsimile."

GEORGE ORWELL
c. 1949

"There is a language learned in the womb that never needs interpreters. It is a frictional electricity that runs between people. It carries the pertinent information without words. Its meanings are 'I find you are incredibly attractive. I can hardly keep my hands off your body.'"[1]

MAYA ANGELOU
from A Song Flung Up to Heaven

Chapter 11

MIGHTY REAL

DECONSTRUCTING FABULOUS

Once the gay man emerges from the shame that has defined so much of his life in stages one and two, he is now faced with the task of deconstructing what was once predicated on the tenants of shame. The parts of his life that are rooted in the practices of avoiding shame, splitting, and achieving inauthentic validation no longer work for him. He moves through life as if he were the rusty tin man, awkward and clumsy, slowed by the excessive weight of leaden limbs.

But how does one function in the world without the familiar ways of being? If he is no longer driven by the desire to taste and touch the newest model of man on the street, how shall he spend his evenings? If his craving for money and success are no longer his favorite, drunken obsession, how will he entertain himself? If he is no longer in the elusive race for the ultimate fashion, where will he spend his energy?

Deconstructing the effects of a life built on the avoidance of and overcompensation for shame is the central process of stage three. Now that shame is no longer the driving force in his life, the structures he so carefully built to avoid shame are no longer needed.

Stage three begins for most gay men with a vague sense of freedom and vacillating awareness of confusion. Everything that is familiar feels somewhat foreign, and there is a growing awareness that life must be slowly redefined in all aspects. It is a time of shuffling that, much like a line of dominos falling, starts with a small change and ends with a radical difference.

Living in Santa Fe, New Mexico, I see more than a few gay men who come to our small town as part of their journey through stage three. They've often lived in the metropolitan "gay ghettos," having lived the life of the urban gay man. Now they are questioning everything, and somehow they are drawn to this dusty New Mexico town where the houses are built of mud and straw at the foot of a mountain. Perhaps, they have wondered, this small town is the antithesis to the pulsating urban gay life of the city and will hold the answers. For some, it does. For others, it does not. Nevertheless, every year a new group of gay men arrives in town, seeking the answers to lives that are no longer based on shame.

Many of these men wander into my psychotherapy office in Santa Fe. I see them often, as they begin to entrust me with the unburdening of their hearts. Each inevitably thinks that his journey from shame to the ambiguity of stage three is unique. And why wouldn't he? His father had no knowledge of this journey, nor did any of his likely role models. How would he know that so many gay men have been this way before?

What always fascinates me is that once a gay man enters into stage three, his visibility in the gay community often diminishes. He is no longer a regular at the gay clubs, nor is he an active player in high gay society. He may, in fact, no longer feel the need to visit the gay ghetto. You may see him on occasion at the gym or at a political fund-raiser, but he is not a regular on the gay scene. This is unfortunate for young men, for they are unable to see the healthy progression from shame to freedom. Many younger gay men just assume that once you get older, you hide out in your house or move away out of embarrassment from having aged. It isn't conceivable to them that many of the gay men who "disappear" do so because they have outgrown the need for the avoidance of shame and acquisition of validation that is at the core of so much of mainstream gay culture.

> "It's as if I developed an aversion to 'gay life.' I started craving a quiet, normal life where I didn't feel I was living onstage."
>
> DARCY FROM HOUSTON, TX

Stage three is akin to the archetype of the wanderer—the man who journeys from his home seeking something better but not certain of what it is he might find. There are many stories down through history of the wanderer, including Homer in the *Iliad* and Moses in the desert. The essence of these stories is also the experience of the gay man in stage three: He embarks on a journey away from a familiar life and seeks a better life for himself. He isn't certain what that better life is, nor is he at all certain that he will ever find it. It is a quest without a defined endpoint.

This is a period of life that is best described as a time of ongoing ambiguity. Nothing is very clear or certain, except that the ways of avoiding shame no longer interest him. Bathhouses, dance clubs, one-night stands, and anonymous sex hold only passing interest for him now. Achieving great financial and career success may still be his goal; but it is a goal that has lost much of its luster and seduction. It now becomes a place to go simply because he hasn't any other attractive alternatives.

The great danger inherent in stage three is that the gay man will foreclose on ambiguity. Rather than allow this lack of clarity to resolve itself naturally, like the settling white flakes in a child's snow globe when it has been put down, he attempts to create artificial clarity and too quickly defines an endpoint to his journey. Or he turns back into the ways of earlier stages, being unwilling to tolerate the ambiguity of the present.

Foreclosure doesn't have to be permanent. Often, it is simply a delay in emotional development simply because it doesn't work. Foreclosure may help alleviate the stress of the moment, but often does not have the power to sustain. The crisis comes roaring back into awareness, and once again, he faces the opportunity to resolve it or choose another form of foreclosure.

Foreclosure, as it can in each of the crises, happens in many different ways. I met Jay five years ago at a dinner party of a mutual friend. Jay was an attractive man, I'd say around forty-two years of age, with dark black hair and a well-trimmed goatee that highlighted his prominent cheekbones beautifully. As I talked to Jay, I learned the fascinating story of his attempt to foreclose on ambiguity. Some years earlier he had ended a decade-long relationship in New York City and moved to Santa Fe. He described it as a period of "purging his soul" and letting go of the mistakes of his past.

Jay spent several years meandering around Santa Fe, working various jobs, and deliberately forming friendships with people he'd never have even noticed before. After a few years of this, he became interested in a well-known spiritual retreat center about a hundred miles away from Santa Fe. As his interest grew, he began to see a way out of his ambiguous dilemma. In short, he thought he had found the ultimate answer that would finally give his life real meaning and purpose. Jay sold everything, including a houseful of beautiful and rare furniture, gave all of his money to the retreat center, and committed to joining the monastery that was associated with the retreat center.

After several years of living as a monk, the day-to-day squabbles among the monks and the business of running a retreat center made him begin to feel increasingly disillusioned with his choice to become a monk. Jay began to wonder if he had been too quick in his decision to join the monastery. It was feeling as if he simply joined a corporation whose only product was spiritual enlightenment—for a price. Two and a half years after joining the monastery and stripping himself of all worldly possessions, he left the monastery penniless, confused, and once again facing the ambiguity from which he had sought to escape by joining the monastery.

Jay's story fascinated me. As I have reflected on that conversation over the years, it became clear to me that Jay's struggle was not unlike the struggles of so many gay men in stage three. He had foreclosed on the ambiguity that he found distressing and escaped into a spiritual practice that he thought would take away the confusion and give him a sense of identity. Fortunately for Jay, he was able to recognize that he had foreclosed, and as painful as it was, he returned to grapple with the true demands of authenticity in stage three. He returned to the mainstream, eventually starting a new relationship and successful career as a ceramic artist.

The way in which Jay foreclosed on stage three was quite dramatic, even for most gay men. However, I see the experience repeated in many different ways by gay men who are desperate to escape the ambiguity of stage three. Take Ben, for example.

Ben was a gay man in his late thirties who had built a very successful publishing business with his partner. While he and his partner had not been lovers for several years, they kept the business together and continued to run it. As you might imagine, running a business with an ex-lover is difficult under the best of circumstances, and it had become something of a nightmare for Ben. One day he invited his partner to a lunch meeting with his attorney and announced that he wanted to be bought out of the business. After almost two years of arguing back and forth, the two reached a settlement price and his former lover bought Ben's share of the company.

With a nice chunk of change and no immediate career goals, Ben spent a year and a half traveling the world to "find himself." He visited all the must-see exotic locations and many an out-of-the-way village that somehow caught his interest. On one such trip, Ben was flying back to Santa Fe and had to change planes in Los Angeles. His flight was delayed and soon after cancelled, so Ben decided to spend a few days roaming around Los Angeles and West Hollywood. On his night stroll down Santa Monica Avenue, he caught the eye of a young man who appeared to be barely twenty years old. He and Ben struck up a conversation and within a few hours were back in Ben's hotel room for the night. The next days were filled with a fast-paced romance that ended with Ben inviting the young man to pack his bags and return to live with him in Santa Fe.

Ben was delighted to have found a new focus in his life and the two of them went about the task of setting up a household together. After six months or so, Ben's new love began complaining about how "quiet" and "small town" Santa Fe felt (it is, without a doubt, a small town in many ways). He started fre-

quenting the clubs with Ben in nearby Albuquerque. In the
year that followed, Ben and his lover went to Albuquerque almost every weekend, drinking heavily and doing surprising
amounts of cocaine and ecstasy. The two of them began picking up other twenty-something men for three-way sex. Ben
wasn't all that wild about it, but I think he felt he had to go
along with it to keep his lover happy. Ben and his lover had met
a handsome young man one night and the three of them began
spending a great deal of time together. Over a period of about a
month, Ben's lover became smitten by their new playmate, and
he pushed Ben to agree to allow the young man to live with
them. Over the next few months, Ben began sensing that his
lover was more interested in the young man than he was in
him. Sure enough, one night at dinner the two of them announced that they were moving out of Ben's house and moving
in together, just the two of them.

Of course, Ben was devastated. All the wagging tongues
around Santa Fe cynically whispered over glasses of fine scotch
and white linen tablecloths, "What did he expect? The guy was
half his age." And, "Ben was a fool if he really thought he would
stick around." Ben was broken-hearted and confused. He
thought he had found the answer to his ambiguity in a sex- and
party-filled relationship. Now he was alone and dazed.

Foreclosure in stage three can happen in many different
ways. Suddenly taking on a new spiritual path, abruptly changing careers or lovers, and moving to a very different kind of city
are just a few of the more common ways. Any way in which you
can imagine giving your life a sudden and radical "make over"
is a way to foreclose from finding happiness and focus from
within.

Foreclosure is not an inevitable part of stage three. Rather, it is a common way of escaping and subsequently prolonging stage three. Some gay men struggle with the ambiguity until it slowly and naturally resolves itself. They wait it out until clarity is theirs and then move forward.

The difference between foreclosure and resolution is distinct. A gay man who forecloses makes an abrupt U-turn in some significant part of his life. He jumps tracks suddenly, expecting that he has "shifted" himself out of the ambiguity into clarity. He has finally found the silver bullet that will slay his demons.

Resolution, on the other hand, comes slowly and is measured. It is a gradual, organic change that seems to flow naturally in life. It needs no sudden jolt or miraculous event. It is a beautiful fractal that emerges out of the chaotic background, slowly revealing itself in the foreground of life.

Resolution is always possible, even when we may have foreclosed earlier. Sometimes we may foreclose on a crisis many times before we are ready to seek resolution. Resolution requires that we tolerate the distress of the crisis long enough to resolve it rather than escape it.

The underlying psychological conflict that is resolved in stage three is the complete acceptance of the self and elimination of toxic shame. Resolution is the manifestation of a gay man who is no longer holding the core belief that he is flawed and unacceptable, and consequently spending most of his energy managing, silencing, and avoiding shame. Instead, he has come to a place of accepting himself as a man who has the potential for both good and evil. He no longer pushes away various parts of himself or hides his shortcomings among many lovers or within the sanctuary of his flawlessly designed home. He embraces it with hard-won acceptance. Here, toxic shame cannot exist.

Because stage three is a place beyond toxic shame, it is also a place of deconstructing and reconstructing the gay man's life. Not with dramatic upheaval as in the jerky moves of foreclosure, but in slow, mindful, and naturally evolving ways. Primarily, this change centers around the parts of his life that were based on shame. Relationships, sexual practices, material appetites, friends, and lifestyle were built during the first two stages as a means to deal with toxic shame. Now those choices no longer seem useful.

Chase had been a moderately successful advertising copy editor back in New York. Now living in a small but sufficient one-bedroom cottage in Key West, he felt he was content. For many years, Key West had been a haven of rest for Chase. The place where he would go to escape the supercharged energy of his New York existence. He had bought the cottage during a few very good years when his bonuses had allowed him to acquire the place with a single signature on a check.

Chase had always loved to cook. Back in New York, he was known for throwing fabulous dinners where, on a good night, one might meet the latest supermodel or artist from Chelsea. Chase loved nothing more than spending all day Saturday shopping and preparing for an extravagant feast to be served later that evening to an equally extravagant gathering of guests.

As Chase turned fifty, he began wonder if there wasn't something more to life than what he'd had. Sure, he'd had some great times along the way, but he couldn't shake the feeling that something fundamental was missing from his life. He'd reached a point in his career where he was making a very good living, but it brought him little satisfaction. He still loved cooking, but the joy of entertaining he once felt was fading away. The thought of sitting around another table while the guests each took turns extolling the latest indulgence they had experienced now bored him beyond description.

Eventually, the time came when the company for whom he worked offered early retirement as a means of cutting costs. Chase thought about it carefully, and eventually took the offer and retired. He sold the New York apartment and headed south to live in his little place in Key West.

Once settled in Key West, he floundered a bit, not sure of what he wanted to do with himself. There were several business opportunities and a few short-lived relationships, but he was far too distracted to commit to anything at the time.

One fall day, he happened to ride his bike past the window of a small local diner that said "for sale." After some thought and a few sleepless nights, he decided to buy the place with the sum he had received for early retirement. It was risky, but it felt like something he really wanted to try.

Years have gone by and he now owns a successful small bistro tucked away on a side street in Key West. It isn't fabulous, has one waiter, and is open only for dinner. His clientele isn't rich or famous, but they are faithful and many have become good friends. More to the point, Chase is finally content.

That's what stage three is all about. Maybe being an ordinary chef in an unremarkable restaurant is really what you want. Or perhaps it is to own a small boat and make a simple living taking tourists out for a snorkel, like Chase's friend Captain Tom does. The point is, stage three is all about letting go of fabulous and being yourself, however glamorous—or not—that is.

Stage three is all about finally achieving authentic validation— the only kind that really satisfies. By showing yourself—your complete self—to the world around you, the world can respond with validation of what is real about you. It doesn't always do so, but when it does, the validation satisfies that deep longing within.

Rage, the emotional product of being unable to achieve authentic validation, begins to dissipate as does all of its disguised expressions. As the authenticity surges, the rage recedes, allowing you to reclaim your life. No longer is your life determined by the fallout of shame and rage. Finally, the freedom to know contentment has arrived.

Chapter 12

HEALING RELATIONSHIP

TRAUMA

I'd been seeing John in therapy for several months. Today, he came into the office with dark circles around his eyes and looking like he'd slept in his clothes.

"Tom left me last night," he mumbled as he slumped into the chair. "Two years, and it's all down the tubes. What is it about me that I can't have a relationship longer than two years?"

John was a successful software engineer who was smart and attractive, but had spent most of his adult years bouncing from relationship to relationship. Now he was thirty-seven and becoming increasingly cynical about relationships. This last relationship with Tom had once again raised his hopes of finding a lifelong lover, only to dash them again as the relationship slowly fizzled. Toward the end, it was clear that Tom's eye had been caught by several other prospects. John did everything he knew to do, but it wasn't enough. Tom eventually left him and moved in with a new boyfriend.

John's life had been like so many of ours. He grew up in a middle-class family with a loving, nurturing mother and a kind but distant father. He knew his father loved him, but they hadn't been close since John's teenage years. When John came out to his parents, they were upset but seemed to get through it fairly well, although they didn't ask about the details of John's life. He introduced his parents to his first live-in lover, but after that relationship fell apart, he avoided telling them much about whom he was seeing. It just made him feel like a double failure: first, he turned out to be gay; and second, he couldn't keep a long-term relationship.

> "After my last relationship broke up, I realized that I had become jaded. I don't think I'll ever meet a man and fall in love like that again."
>
> FRANK FROM BOSTON, MA

John is like so many of us. We are attracted to men, but can't seem to maintain close, honest relationships with the ones we love. It's like we're characters in some horrible nightmare or *film noir*, where the main character is attracted to the one thing he can't seem to ever have.

The roots of our trauma with men come from two distinct sources: being a man in a hypermasculine culture and being a gay man in a decidedly straight world. The two of these combined turn the tables dramatically against us and make having a healthy relationship extremely difficult. We must relearn everything we know about relationships in order to make them work successfully.

WHAT IT MEANS TO BE A MAN

Sadly, our culture raises men to be strong and silent. Straight or gay, the pressure is on from the time we are very young to become our culture's John Wayne–style of man:

- The more pain I can take, the more of a man I am.
- Showing feelings is for women.
- The more I can drink, the manlier I am.
- Intimacy is sex; sex is intimacy.
- Only women depend on others.
- A man takes care of himself without help from others.
- No one can hurt you if you are strong.
- I am what I earn.
- It is best to keep your problems to yourself.
- Winning is all that really matters.

Where did this stuff come from? It's everywhere in our society, from the movie heroes we love to the politicians we vote for. Our culture demands that men fit into a tightly defined role.

As gay men, we like to think that we've exempted ourselves from all of this macho stereotyping. After all, we've committed the *great* masculine transgression of falling in love with another man.

Truth is, those masculine stereotypes are as much a part of the fabric of our lives as they are for straight men. We may have rejected some or even most of it on the surface, but we first learned our behavior patterns—particularly those relating to emotions—like all men, from our fathers.

Our fathers exerted enormous influence over our lives. For most of our young years, we wanted to be just like our fathers. Once we got into the teenage years, much of that reversed, and we resented much of what our fathers did and said. Resentment and admiration are always two sides of the same coin.

Your first and most powerful model for how to be a man was your father. Like it or not, you absorbed many of his ways of dealing with the world. There never has been and never will be a man who will have such a strong influence over your life as your father does.

As a young gay man, the relationship with your father became a template from which your relationships with all other men would come. What you craved from him was love, affection, and tenderness. As we have seen, what most of us received from our fathers was far less.

We needed our fathers to give us a loving model of a male relationship. Instead, what we got was the best that they could give under the circumstances, which was far less than what we needed as gay boys.

Our mothers were a different story. They were more often nurturing and loving (this, too, is an enforced cultural norm for women). As we grew older, they too sensed our differences and tried to make up for our pain by giving us extra attention and care. They saw their husbands perplexed by the son who wasn't like all the other boys, and often they tried to compensate for his further emotional detachment.

For many of us, this meant that we grew up receiving most of or all of the affection and tenderness we needed from our mothers, and very little from our fathers. This kind of relationship with a woman is wonderful, but it left a huge hole in our experience with men. Where were we going to learn how to relate to a man in a tender, loving, and honest way? Where was our role model for maintaining a lasting relationship between men (without the intervention of a woman)?

As a result, gay men were unable as children and adolescents to have a close parental relationship with the gender they would grow to find erotic. To understand the enormous disadvantage this caused you, think about how it worked for young straight men.

They were able to have a close relationship with a nurturing individual of the gender to which they were attracted. While it didn't
always make them better at relationships, they had a template for
what a close, loving relationship would be with their wives.

In addition, women are taught in our culture to be the care-
takers of relationships. They are expected to be the ones to nurture their husband and compensate for his lack of emotional disclosure. In most cases, it is the woman in a straight relationship
that does the lion's share of creating and maintaining a warm
sense of love and home.

What this all suggests is that we were at a severe disadvantage
for successful relationships. Not only were we deprived of a
model of a tender, honest, and loving relationship between men,
we also didn't have the "emotional safety net" that a woman creates in a straight relationship. Nor were we given the social as-
signment and skills for nurturing and maintaining intimate relationships as women are.

And the news only gets worse. When we finally met another
man and fell in love, he was just as likely struggling in stage one
or two as we were. All the behaviors we used in stage one, such
as splitting, had traumatic effects on our relationships. We were
prone to such relationship-damaging behaviors as betrayal and
emotional dishonesty.

In addition to being two wounded and struggling men, we
didn't have the support that all new relationships need and that
straight relationships almost always receive. There were no
clergy to advise us on the importance of staying together. For
many of us, our parents weren't of much help, either. Family
gatherings with our new partner were generally more a struggle
than a celebration of our union. Even our closest friends weren't

always supportive of the new relationship, jealous of the time and attention we diverted from them toward our new love.

The cards were stacked for failure. All these factors converged upon us, making our first romantic endeavor highly unlikely to survive the test of time. We weren't prepared to have a relationship with another man, especially not another man who was similarly wounded. We struggled and hoped for the best, but for most of us, those first relationships failed after the blush of new love had faded away.

> "I'll never forget that the day after I left my lover of ten years he said to me: 'You married your father.' It hit me like a boulder. In one instant I knew he was right, and in the same instant I was disgusted and ashamed of myself. I had prided myself in not being like my parents. I was educated, liberated, and free from their small world, or so I thought. But here I was, at forty, living the same relationships they had lived. How did this happen?"
>
> ROBERT FROM NEW ORLEANS, LA

MARRYING OUR FATHERS

Flawed as it may have been, most of us used the closest experience we had as the role model for an honest and loving relationship with a man—our relationship with our fathers. It was our only guide to what a male-to-male relationship might be.

Of course, none of this was conscious. We simply fell in love with a man who seemed comfortable and familiar. On some level, of course, he reminded us of our father. Perhaps he looked and acted different, but underneath it all there were certain key characteristics that recalled feelings of safety and adoration.

In the course of psychotherapy, more than a few gay men have been amazed to realize how close many of their ex-lovers' personality characteristics were to their father's. It may have never occurred to you, too, that this is what has occurred in your life. Ask yourself: Was my father emotionally withdrawn? Judgmental? Physically abusive? If so, have your lovers been cut from the

same fabric? Coming to terms with this may be a big step for you in breaking the cycle of failed relationships.

All too often, we marry our fathers. Unfortunately, it's the only model we have of a close male relationship. So when you see your father in another man who finds you attractive, you marry him. It's familiar and safe, so you take refuge in it. You feel like you've known your lover all your life. That's because, in a very real sense, you have.

INNOCENCE LOST

A gay man's first romantic relationship with another man is almost as influential in our lives as our relationship with our fathers. The excitement of allowing your-

"I've been lying to everyone for most of my life. I lied to Tom, my best friend in high school, when he asked me if I was a queer. I lied to every girlfriend who I used to prove to myself that I wasn't gay. I lied to my parents about who I was dating, what my life was really like, or even when I would get married. I've lied to my employers, my doctor, and even the priest at my parents' church by playing like I was straight. I've lied to every lover I've had about being monogamous when I wasn't. I guess I sound like some kind of monster, but I'm really not. I don't think I'm any different than every other gay guy on the street, either. We're all screwing around. But then, I think that's just what men do."

JEFFREY FROM PALO ALTO, CA

self to freely love another man. The freedom of finally allowing yourself to have what you want. The joy of sexual fulfillment. The closeness of male companionship. The ecstasy of new love. All of these things converge in that first romantic relationship, giving it

"At first we were really happy to-gether. It was the first time either of us had been in a relationship with a man and definitely the first time either of us had lived with a lover. It was such a rush to come home at night and have him wait-ing there. No sneaking around. We could do whatever we wanted to-gether. Then, I'm not sure when it happened—it wasn't any particu-lar day—we started to grow apart. Every now and then I'd meet someone at the gym and we'd mess around. I was pretty sure he was doing the same with guys he met on the road. We never really talked about it. Just one day, I came home a day early from a business trip and found him in bed with a really cute guy I'd seen around. I was completely devas-tated. I guess I didn't have any right to be since I had been fool-ing around too, but I was. I've never been the same since, and certainly never trusted another man to be faithful."

FRANK FROM
SAN FRANCISCO, CA

exceptional power to imprint upon our lives like no other rela-tionship ever will again.

Two wounded men, both struggling to discover themselves and desperately lacking in skills and role models, come together to find love. It is a tragic recipe filled with momentous highs and devastating lows.

That first relationship, for most gay men, ends in disaster. It is one of the most common sto-ries gay men tell in therapy: the traumatic loss of innocence they experienced during their first gay relationship. After that relation-ship fails and subsequent rela-tionships thereafter, you begin to look at men differently. The seeds of cynicism and bitterness are planted deep in your heart. You start to lose faith that loving rela-tionships can exist between men.

Some gay men even go back into the closet after that first re-lationship falls apart. They may even find the first available woman and decide to marry her. Why? Because the pain of that first gay relationship falling apart only confirms the fear that a gay man can never have a happy life and committed relationship. At least with a woman a man can create a stable family, even if a woman isn't what he really wants. The promise of stability, commitment, societal approval, and family is a very strong lure in the face of trying to blaze a difficult trail with another man, where none of those things comes easily.

Those of us who didn't retreat decided to eventually try again with another man. We did, and found ourselves once again struggling with the same issues. Maybe this time or the time after that we resolutely decided to make compromises. We were going to do whatever it took to make it work. It became an all-consuming challenge to make our relationship survive despite the odds against us.

There is an extremely important lesson to learn here. *Two deeply emotionally wounded people cannot form a healthy relationship.* They may struggle, compromise, and even stay together, but until they each heal their own wounds, the relationship will always be a struggle.

Those first failed relationships stole our innocence from us. In most cases it was not a sexual innocence, but a wonderful trusting innocence about what kind of relationship we could have with our lovers. Without any role models of successful, happy, and loving gay relationships, we slowly begin to lose hope that such a thing exists. There's no doubt that we still crave it, but so many of us lost the hope that we would ever satisfy that craving.

In fact, the lost innocence convinced many among us that being in a relationship made things *worse*, not better. The only way to be happy was to be single and emotionally unattached to the men with whom we have sex. That way, we would no longer be hurt and disappointed when the relationship inevitably failed.

The bitterness and cynicism that emerge from failed relationships can be seen in almost all of popular gay culture. In some gay circles, men have given up on long-term relationships altogether, instead choosing to settle for the occasional short-term hookup. All of this naturally emerges from the hearts of men who have not only given up the hope of having a fulfilling relationship, but are also actively seeking sexual release without emotional involvement.

Stage three is the time in a gay man's life when he begins to reflect on the relationship trauma he has experienced. As the research on trauma grows, there is an increasing awareness on the very real effects of relational trauma on a person. Two important facts, among others, have emerged from this body of research. First, there is growing evidence that emotional memories rarely fade. The well-known neuroscientist J.E. LeDoux has written "emotional memory may be forever."[1] Experiences that involve extreme and significant emotional responses are likely imprinted in our neurological pathways in significantly different ways. These pathways show great resiliency and maintain their potency regardless of age, thus allowing a person to re-

"Craig and I were in the same fraternity at the University of Alabama. We spent a lot of time together our freshman year, since we were both pre-law majors. It wasn't until our sophomore year that we started sleeping together. For the first year or so, we both had to get really drunk and then play like we didn't know what we were doing. By the time we were seniors, we had moved out of the frat house and lived in our own apartment. Nobody suspected what was happening between us and we kept dating girlfriends to keep up appearances, or so I thought. We'd drop off our dates and then head back to the apartment and have sex.

"It must have been after spring break when Craig came home and just out of the blue tells me he's member emotionally significant events from even early childhood for most, if not all, of one's life.

The second important fact about relationship trauma is that emotional memories dramatically affect the way in which we process similar stimuli after the trauma. For example, if you were a passenger during an almost fatal car accident, you will like respond differently to a car for the rest of your life. If the accident occurred as the result of an oncoming car swerving into your lane while driving at night, you are likely to respond with sudden anxiety to oncoming headlights that may appear to even slightly venture toward your lane.

These two facts bear important information for the gay man who experiences relationship trauma. First, the memories of that trauma remain fresh and active throughout his life, and second, he is likely to react to future relationships based on these traumatic memories.

getting married. I was so depressed that I flunked one of my final exams and had to retake the course during that summer. Craig never talked about what had happened. 'How could he be so cruel?' I remember thinking. I would have done anything to win him back.

"Craig got married that summer, and after the wedding, I never heard from him again. I know that's what pushed me into getting married. It confirmed all my fears about gay relationships—all the 'it isn't natural and it will never work' stuff. It wasn't until ten years later, after Glenda and I divorced, that I finally came out of the closet. Can you believe it? One man set my life back ten years!"

RAY FROM ATLANTA, GA

Dean discovered that his boyfriend of seven years was having an affair with his best friend. Not only was he having an affair, but it had been going on for several years. Dean was devastated by the experience. Some time passed before he would consider being in a relationship again, and when Dean did finally find another relationship, he was extremely suspicious of his new boyfriend whenever they weren't together. When his boyfriend's friends whom Dean had not met would call, Dean would become increasingly jealous and almost always end up in a fight with his boyfriend. Not only had his memories of the betrayal not faded, but he was entering his new relationship by carrying with him the response elicited by his past betrayal.

It is rare that a gay man makes it from young adulthood into middle age without suffering at least moderate relationship trauma. The odds are stacked wildly against the possibility that even the most well-adjusted gay man would choose to be in a relationship with another well-adjusted gay man. It rarely happens. And so, two wounded men come together in what starts as a loving union and often ends in a traumatic and heart-wounding separation.

By the time the gay man reaches stage three, he is keenly aware that he has some difficult problems handling relationships. For some gay men, this realization can become primary in their awareness, triggering feelings of depression and hopelessness about ever finding the love that they need. In stage three he accepts that he has experienced past relationship trauma, and sets about to find a way to diminish its effects on his life.

WHAT IS TRAUMA?

Over the past few decades there has been a lot of talk about psychological trauma, and for good reason. Much of it began shortly after the return of soldiers from the Vietnam War. Many of these men had seen horrendous acts of violence and had been terrified for the safety of their lives on more than one occasion. After returning to the United States, they seemed to have great difficulty acclimating into normal society. Many couldn't seem to hold a job, others became chronic substance abusers, and still others seemed to fall into a tenacious depression that just wouldn't relent as depression normally does. In large part, it was the concern of these veterans that raised the awareness about the lasting effects of trauma.

Recent research into trauma has identified some specific biological effects of trauma. Several findings show that among patients who have experienced significant psychological trauma, the hippocampal region in the brain has as much as twelve percent less volume than those who have not experienced such trauma.[2]

Relationship trauma, however, is usually a significantly different experience from that of trauma caused by life-threatening events. What is curious about the connect between these two different types of trauma is the commonality in basic symptoms. The experience of psychological trauma, as is typically diagnosed (posttraumatic stress disorder [PTSD]), has at least some of the following symptoms:

- Reliving the trauma: This can happen through nightmares, flashbacks, or reexperiencing as a result of being in the presence of stimuli reminiscent of the traumatic event.
- Efforts to avoid thoughts or feelings that are associated with the trauma.
- Efforts to avoid activities or situations that arouse memories of the trauma.
- Inability to remember some important aspect of the trauma (psychogenic amnesia).
- Marked reduced interest in important activities.

- Feeling of a lack of interest or expulsion by others.
- Limited affect; such as inability to cherish loving feelings.
- A feeling of not having any future (foreshortened future); not expecting to have a career, get married, have children, or live a long life.
- Hypervigilance (heightened sensitivity to possible traumatic stimuli).

Gay men who have experienced significant or repeated relationship trauma often exhibit many of these same symptoms in their relationships. For example, they often relive the trauma in their dreams or imagine that the trauma is happening again. They often report not being able to remember, for example, what the fight was really about or what happened after they discovered an infidelity. They very often anticipate the inevitable end of the relationship (foreshortened future) even when things have been going well or the trauma is from a previous relationship. They have a heightened awareness of relationship trauma and may overreact to events they imagine may lead to trauma, and depression of some degree is almost always present.

> "After John had the affair, I would wake up in the middle of the night in a sweat after dreaming that I was in the room watching the two of them go at it. As hard as I tried to put it behind me, the dreams kept coming."
>
> LALO FROM SAN FRANCISCO, CA

The presence of relationship trauma often makes it difficult, and sometimes impossible, for the sufferer to experience a satisfying relationship. He is constantly scanning the relationship environment for signs of betrayal or abuse, and this expenditure of energy alone transforms a relationship from a satisfying experience into a very tiring job. And as you might imagine, it's no piece of cake to live with a man who interprets even small things as relationship-destroying or who privately assumes that the relationship will not exist in the future. Sadly, the relationship trauma victim often behaves in such as way as to elicit more rejection and even trauma from those around him.

There are as many twisted ways to be traumatized by a relationship as there are curses in mouths of men. However, there are some common patterns in the trauma experienced by gay men. What follows is a dictionary of the relationship traumas experienced by most gay men. Each type of trauma represents a different experience, and consequently, the ongoing symptoms of each are different. There are four primary types of relationship trauma experienced by gay men:

- Betrayal
- Abuse
- Abandonment
- Relationship Ambivalence

Betrayal

Without question, the most devastating form of relationship trauma is betrayal. More than pain of lost love and dreams, it almost always revolves around a deliberate act of one partner to undermine, deceive, or destroy the other partner. The devastation it leaves behind can take years, and in some cases, a lifetime, to heal.

What makes betrayal so searingly hurtful is that it involves planned deception between two men who ostensibly trust each other. It goes beyond destroying the relationship—it calls into question one's ability to perceive reality correctly and to judge the character of another person. Once one man has been seriously betrayed by another man—a man with whom he also shares a bed, food, money, and life—all men become fundamentally unsafe. If he cannot protect himself from someone whom he knows so well, then who can be trusted? If another man proclaims to love me and simultaneously plots to deceive me, what is the meaning of love? Does it exist or is it just a cruel fantasy?

Betrayals rarely develop overnight. A betrayal is often the product of a long series of small deceptions, pretexts, and omissions that eventually add up to something much larger. The betrayer slowly acclimates to small white lies, and then progresses on to larger, more deceptive schemes.

The betrayer always has a handy rationalization. Oftentimes, his rationalization is based on something that is true. In his frustration and anger, he uses this fact as a license to do something he perceives to be of equal harm. As the betrayal grows, it spins beyond the initiating circumstance, eventually achieving a life and energy of its own.

The most common form of betrayal is that of infidelity in a monogamous relationship between men. It takes, however, more than just a sexual indiscretion to make for betrayal. Betrayal may start as such, but it eventually becomes sexual and emotional duplicity.

Peter was about twenty-eight when he first visited South Beach. He and his lover had saved their money for months and planned the trip carefully. They had researched the latest hot spots for gay men in South Florida and arrived with both a determination and excitement to have a knock-out time.

On the first day, Peter was laying on the beach by 9 a.m. His lover had a brief business appointment that morning and

agreed to join him around lunchtime. Not long after Peter settled into his rectangle of sun in the middle of the gay section
beach, he met Ignacio, a dark-haired, slightly overweight, friendly
man of about thirty-five. Peter and Ignacio struck up a conversation that soon led to the two of them heading off to Ignacio's
Lincoln Avenue condo.

The late-morning rendezvous had been a very welcome release for Peter, since the sex between him and his lover had lately
become somewhat routine and perfunctory. He felt twinges of
guilt over the fling, but decided that he would return to the
beach by lunch and keep the whole affair to himself.

Over the week in Miami, Peter and Ignacio found several ex-
cuses to get together. When Peter's lover wanted to go shopping
at the local Saks Fifth Avenue, Peter said that he was too relaxed
and wanted to stay at the hotel and nap. No sooner had his lover
exited the terrazzo steps of the boutique hotel in which they were
staying, than Peter had Ignacio on his cell phone. Half an hour
later, he was back in Ignacio's apartment.

Not only had Peter found Ignacio to be a great lover, he was
also a physician at the local hospital, and from what Peter could
surmise, did quite well. The two of them had really hit it off, and
as the week drew to a close, it became clear that both Peter and
Ignacio were quite taken with each other.

On the plane ride home to Dallas, Peter found himself sinking
into a hopeless depression and desperately wanting to see Ignacio again. Once back at home, he called Ignacio and was delighted and relieved to hear his voice on the other end.

That night at dinner, less than four hours after stepping off the
airplane, Peter told his lover everything. After he admitted to the
affair of the past week, he dropped another bombshell. He was
leaving tomorrow to return to Miami and live with Ignacio.

At times of great surprise, we often grow numb and begin to see things with a clarity of purpose that we haven't seen before. Peter's lover, feeling just such numbness, was upset but told Peter that he would help him pack. The next morning, he gave Peter a few thousand dollars and dropped him off at the airport.

It took weeks before the enormity of the betrayal really hit Peter's lover. He could hardly grasp the reality. One day he was embarking on a much anticipated vacation with the man he loved, and seven days later he was bidding him good-bye and into the arms of another man. In a mere week, everything he had built his life around seemed to collapse. He could have understood, although it would have hurt him, that Peter had had a "roll in the hay" with a handsome Cuban doctor, but what he couldn't understand now was that Peter had actually allowed himself to fall in love with another man. He thought back to the dinners he and Peter had enjoyed in the sidewalk cafés of South Beach. All the while, he was having a great vacation, and Peter was falling in love with another man. Peter had acted as if he were having a wonderful vacation, and he had been stupid enough to think that it was because the two of them were together in wonderful, sunny paradise.

Was it that the doctor has more money? Was it because he wasn't attractive to Peter anymore? Had their whole relationship been just one big charade?

It's always surprising to me how many gay men come to therapy reporting just this kind of blatant and cutting betrayal that they experienced at the hands of a former lover. Of course, betrayal is not unique to gay men by any means, but it does seem to be a serious problem in most gay relationships. One gay therapist I know says, "Second only to HIV, betrayal is the most devastating gay epidemic." One hallmark symptom of a gay man who has experienced betrayal is *relationship hopelessness.*

Relationship hopelessness is present when a gay man no longer believes that a relationship can be a fulfilling endeavor. He may have crushes, infatuations, and flings, but he never allows them to develop into a long-term relationship. A week, a month, or six months at most are all he will give to another man. The gay man suffering from relationship hopelessness looks cynically at his friends who are in a long-term relationship and imagines all of the torture and pain they must be enduring. He prides himself on having achieved something of a more rational stance by not seeking a relationship.

Relationship hopelessness is truly widespread among gay men. There are even some gay men, such as those involved in Queer Nation or the Radical Faeries, who suggest that gay men are not meant to be in committed relationships. Among other things, they point to other animal species where the males never remain with the same female, and suggest that men are just genetically programmed to be "poly-amorous."

When I encounter such relationship hopelessness in a gay male client, we can almost always work together to discover at least one and often multiple betrayals in his relationships with male lovers. It most cases, the betrayals are quite clear and vivid in the client's memory.

The work of healing betrayal is at the same time simple and complex. The simplicity of the work to be done is that it revolves around one principle: acceptance. The complexity lies in the innate difficulty that all human beings have in accepting those things that do not fit into our expectations of the world around us.

The acceptance of betrayal is about accepting the following:

1. All men, and gay men in particular, have shortcomings.

2. Betrayal is a product of the betrayer's woundedness and not the fault of the betrayed.

The underlying dynamic of this acceptance is the realization that betrayal has a predictable and knowable cause: emotional woundedness. If we wish to have a relationship that is free of betrayal, then we must either find a partner who is not wounded or find a partner who is willingly and actively working on his own emotional wounds. Of course, the former is difficult if not impossible to find. The latter becomes the requirement of all gay men who wish to heal their relationship trauma.

When we accept that the betrayal we have experienced results from another person's wounds, we free ourselves from the otherwise automatic back draft of self-doubt and invalidation. It is not we who have created the betrayal, but rather it was something that was done to us, quite independent of our own actions.

The question shifts from "What did I do to deserve this?" to "How can I prevent this from happening again?" Acceptance allows us to move on to prevention and regain a sense of control over our lives. Of course, we can never prevent betrayal completely, but we can make great strides in decreasing its likelihood without sacrificing our hope in relationships.

It is a fundamental dialectical dilemma: We are not responsible for the betrayal we experience, and at the same time, we can work toward preventing it. On the surface, the two seem to cancel each other out. If you look a bit closer, however, you'll find that there is synthesis of these two seemingly opposing truths, and in that synthesis lies healing.

The acceptance of betrayal is two-sided. Not only do we accept that the betrayal is the result of another man's woundedness, but there is also the implied acceptance that if another man is not so wounded, he is less likely to betray us. If emotional wounds can cause betrayal, then the absence of these same wounds is likely to prevent betrayal.

Until now, we have spoken of the betrayed and the betrayer as two separate individuals. However, in real life they are often the same person. The man who betrays in one circumstance is also the betrayed in another circumstance. Truth is, a gay man has likely been both betrayer and the betrayed in his relationships. He has both given and received of this vitriolic cocktail.

Given this, the work of acceptance takes on a life-size proportion. We accept not only that the betrayal we experienced resulted from another's wounds *but that the betrayal we perpetrated was the result of our own wounds.*

As you might expect, relationship hopelessness comes not only from having been betrayed but also from knowing that within you lies the capability of betraying. How can you trust another man not to betray you when you have been willing to betray? When we overcome the shame of stage three and begin to carefully examine the parts of ourselves that were previously hidden by shame, we see that we are capable of inflicting great pain upon our lovers. We have been both perpetrator and victim of emotional violence within our relationships.

How can a gay man trust that he is no longer willing to commit betrayal in his relationships? How can he trust himself not to destroy those he loves? The answer comes from the resolution of toxic shame that occurred in stage three. When he is no longer driven by the avoidance of shame, he no longer employs the tactics of shame avoidance.

This translates into a gay man who no longer needs to run into the arms of another man to soothe a deep sense of shame. He no longer must prove his worth and sexual validity by seeking out sexual gratification with partners outside the boundaries of his relationship. While the interest in sexual exploits remains, his desire and willingness to act upon this urge diminishes dramatically. In other words, he may get excited at the prospect of new sexual partners, but he is not blinded by a craving for sexual validation as he may have been previously. Perhaps it might be a good time, but now there are other considerations that are more important to him.

Eventually, the gay man begins to trust himself again. He can have a relationship and not automatically destroy it. He can choose a partner who cherishes him and will not destroy him in return.

Abuse

Much has been written about domestic abuse in heterosexual relationships, and virtually all of it applies to gay men. We are no strangers to our share of physical, emotional, and sexual abuse. The gay man's experience of abuse is heightened by the fact that we are men, and men should be able to protect themselves from harm. All too often, the gay man is embarrassed to report physical abuse.

Sexual abuse is also all too common. A sizable minority of gay men were sexually abused as children, and an even larger number report at least one rape-like experience in their past.

Gay men tend to resist labeling forced sexual behavior as abuse. They may hold themselves responsible for having picked up the hitchhiker or the handsome boy at the gym. Who do they have but themselves to blame for what happens after that?

Many gay men have a difficult time identifying their own childhood sexual experiences as sexual abuse. I often hear, "I wanted it." Or "I just remember being scared and turned on."

Regardless of how it is rationalized, all of these experiences are sexual abuse, and while not every instance of abuse creates symptoms of trauma, many do. Because the symptoms of trauma are often felt long after the traumatic event, it is common for the victim of sexual abuse not to make the connection between the injury and the symptom. With some work and the guidance of a psychotherapist, the gay man can often identify these connections and come to an awareness of how his life has been adversely affected by sexual abuse.

One symptom that is sometimes seen among survivors of childhood sexual abuse is the tendency in later life to use sex as a way of attracting other people or getting what you want. Surveys of adolescent hustlers bear out the facts: most adolescents and young men who are in the sex trade were sexually abused at a younger age. Sex is learned as a way of controlling other people or as a way of attracting people who will care for you.

"I met the guy in the mall restroom when I was there with my girlfriend. He had the bluest eyes and most chiseled body I'd ever seen. We made a plan and I dropped my girlfriend off at her house, then headed over to the address he had given me. I was so excited—I hadn't had many experiences with men and certainly not with a sex god like this man. He met me at the door with a robe on that was open in the front. Once in the bedroom, he overpowered me, tied me up, and penetrated me. All I remember was wondering if I would get out of there alive."

GEORGE FROM BETHESDA, MD

One night sitting around a lovely pool in Fort Lauderdale, a friendly and apparently successful gay man—I'll call him John—told the story of his paper routes as a young boy. He was now a handsome man and looked as if he had been a very attractive boy when he was younger. He recalled how he would make his rounds of delivering the paper every day, and once a month he would stop by each house to collect the bill. At one house, a man answered the door (the father of a neighborhood friend) and invited him in. Once in the house, the man removed his shorts and began fondling himself. John remembers finding this very exciting and equally terrifying. The man then took my friend into his bedroom and sodomized him.

John told the story of running home, taking a shower, and of being scared to death that anyone would find out what had happened. When John approached the man's house the next month, the same thing happened. In the years that followed, my friend recalled the story of how he started wearing tight cutoff shorts when he went bill collecting and how he would make a sport of how many men he could seduce. Over a few years, he recalls having regular sexual encounters with a dozen men on his paper route.

When the time came for college, John had decided that he wanted to go to medical school. He was certainly smart enough, but his family didn't have the money for all those years of schooling, so he covered his extra expenses by having sex for money. By the time he was accepted into medical school, he had a regular clientele of men who paid him well for the time he spent with them.

I was amazed, as you might be, to hear this story of a boy who hustled his way through medical school. I was even more amazed that John recounted the story with virtually no acknowledgement that it was unusual, much less abusive. He laughed as he recounted such things as the number of his friends' fathers that he slept with during those years. Everyone else laughed with him.

It's impossible to say conclusively that the two are related, but I can't help but notice that John has never really been able to maintain a committed, long-term relationship as an adult. His current relationship has existed for three years—the longest one to date—but, by his own admission, only because he and his lover have sex with other men. There are times when either one of them will go out for the evening and not return home until the next day, having spent the night with another man he found attractive.

The effects of childhood sexual abuse can have more severe consequences for a gay man. A sizeable number of all people who are sexually abused in childhood have extreme difficulty regulating their emotions as adults. Such adult diagnoses as Borderline Personality Disorder and Dissociative Identity Disorder are known to have strong links to childhood sexual abuse. Other problems like substance abuse, suicidal behavior, deliberate self-harm, and even antisocial (criminal) behavior have also been linked to childhood sexual abuse.

The effects of sexual activity, regardless of the child's desire or participation, are significant and damaging. A child is quite capable of strong sexual feelings but at the same time is not capable of handling the emotional aftermath of such feelings. The introduction of sexual activity too early in a child's or adolescent's life interferes with his ability to develop adequate and appropriate coping mechanisms. What may have seemed like a harmless and even highly erotic act is often devastating psychologically.

There is also an interesting phenomenon that exists among some survivors of violent childhood sexual abuse. As adults, they *prefer* violent sexual acts, and may even be unable to achieve an erection unless there is a feeling of violence or force during sex. They seek out others to bind, whip, chain, and otherwise brutalize themselves. For these men, the pleasure of sex has been almost inextricably linked with violence. They have highly eroticized memories of sexual violence and often fantasize about "rough sex."

Sexual abuse experienced as an adult is often not nearly as damaging as it is to the child, but it, too, has lasting effects. More than a few gay men have reported that they are exclusively a "top" because of a violent or forceful rape in the past.

The gay male perpetrator of sexual abuse is almost always seeking control or reenacting childhood sexual experiences. He may feel helpless and out of control in life or in his relationship. Or he may have eroticized violence and mistakenly assumed that others secretly fantasize about sexual violence, too.

Abandonment

Abandonment is not unique to gay men, nor are any other forms of relationship trauma. Still, I am always taken aback by the stories of gay men who have been suddenly and utterly abandoned by their partners. It's the old melodrama of the husband who goes to work and runs off with his secretary, never returning home. The wife finds out from a letter, a phone call, or the nosy neighbor who's just heard the latest gossip.

Abandonment is so deeply wounding because it allows no room for closure and leaves myriad unanswered questions. What went wrong? Why didn't you say something earlier? How did I not see it coming? What did I do to drive you away?

The gay man who suddenly abandons his partner almost always does so because of a secondary emotion of shame. When he feels angry in the relationship, it immediately goes into shame for feeling angry. When he senses the relationship failing, he is subsequently overcome with shame at the failure. He cannot talk

with his partner about the problems because he feels so much shame about his role in creating the problems. No matter what is happening in the relationship, his final response is shame.

Obviously, this becomes unbearable. He cannot see a way out of the misery until another opportunity comes into his life. He suddenly takes a job in another city, moves in with a new

> "I came home from work and noticed that something looked different, more vacant. Then I realized that some of the furniture was gone. It took me a while, but I finally realized that Randy had taken all of his stuff out of the house. Just like that, nine years of being together were suddenly over."
>
> TERRY FROM LITTLE ROCK, AR

boyfriend, or moves out of the house when his partner is out of town. Because he cannot face the overwhelming shame of admitting the problems and working through them, he runs away. Whether it is into the arms of another man or to a new town, he finds a convenient excuse to escape the tyranny of his own toxic shame.

The aftereffects of abandonment are devastating for the abandoned. In the vacuum created by unanswered questions and unresolved feelings, he almost always turns inward and blames himself for the abandonment. Even the most confident gay men find themselves undermined and confused.

A unique form of abandonment occurs when a gay man abandons his partner emotionally. He withdraws into himself and begins to live a private life, one that is separate from his relationship. He suppresses, masks, and blunts his emotions when around his partner, presenting a skewed version of himself to his partner.

It's not unusual for the gay man who emotionally withdraws to privately complain that his partner doesn't understand him, and, therefore, wonder what's the point of revealing his true thoughts and feelings to him. And while this may be true, now that he is withdrawn, what choice does the partner have but to not understand him?

Emotional withdrawal is often triggered by perceived invalidation within a relationship. Perceived invalidation can come in many forms, but the end result is the feeling that your partner doesn't understand or isn't willing to see your side of the story. It can be as simple as the gay man who makes pasta every week, oblivious to the fact that his partner doesn't like pasta and who sees this as an invalidating act. Or as big as the gay man who tells his partner what an idiot he's been for having been in an automobile accident. Regardless of the cause, perceived invalidation on a regular basis elicits emotional withdrawal. Eventually, the invalidated gay man shuts down completely.

Emotional abandonment is a two-edged sword. Not only is it traumatic for the person who is abandoned, but it often comes out of distress experienced by the one who abandons. The abandoned man feels lonely, isolated, and rejected. Ironically, the man who abandons usually feels the same.

Emotional abandonment is often the precursor to sexual and physical abandonment. First, the gay man stops sharing his most cherished feelings with his partner. Then, slowly, he loses interest in sex. If the cycle isn't broken, he eventually is likely to abandon the partner altogether, leaving both feeling as if they never really knew each other at all.

The Ambivalent Relationship

A more subtle kind of relationship trauma is created by being in a relationship with a man who at times is warm and caring, but once he senses that his partner is drawing closer to him emotionally, he backs off and becomes emotionally distant and removed. Don't be fooled by the lack of drama inherent in this kind of trauma—in the long run, it can be just as wounding as the other forms of relationship trauma.

The ambivalent relationship between gay men is a relationship where one partner woos and seduces the other partner by showing his tender and vulnerable side. Once the other is drawn into his shower of affection and attention, he backs away and becomes distant, and perhaps even critical of the other. Once he senses that he may lose the other man, he again shows such enticing attributes as compassion, humility, or sexual interest. Once the other is secured back into the relationship, he withdraws again. This on-again, off-again approach-avoidant behavior continues, often for years, confusing and disorienting the emotions of the recipient of this treatment.

The traumatic wounding that this created in the ambivalent relationship is a slow but steady process that causes the recipient to question his ability to function in the relationship. At its worst, it is truly crazy-making, causing him to question his own hold on reality.

The primary source of emotional validation is usually a man's significant other. When he is angry about anything in life, he expresses his frustration and anger to his partner and looks for validation of his feelings. The partner may agree that this situation is indeed frustrating and his anger is justified. Or the partner may disagree and invalidate the emotion of anger. In a close intimate relationship between gay men, they often look to each other for validation of their most significant emotions.

In the ambivalent relationship, the gay man's emotions are sometimes validated and sometimes not. This can create growing confusion and cause him to question his own thoughts and feelings. It puts him off-balance, and he is never quite certain why some emotions are validated only at certain times. One day he is the apple of his lover's eye; the next, his lover acts as if he were not even around. It is disarming, and it causes even the most secure gay man to question his ability to understand and navigate relationships.

Dan came to me for psychotherapy several years ago. He had been in a relationship with a man for more than ten years. What Dan described in our first sessions was clearly an ambivalent relationship. Dan's lover, Mark, traveled frequently for business. At times, he would be on the road for weeks. During some trips, Mark would call every night to talk with Dan. During other trips, Dan would receive only one quick phone call or possibly not hear from Mark. Sometimes when Mark would return from a trip, he seemed eager to reconnect with Dan. Other times, it was as if he looked right through him.

Dan also described times when the two of them would go out to parties. Mark could be very attentive to Dan prior to going out, but when they arrived at the party, Mark was off on his own. Dan even noticed that his conversation changed. Instead of saying things like, "We just bought a house," he would say, "I just bought a house."

At first, Dan imagined that maybe Mark was having an affair. After all, he was out of town a great deal—the perfect setup for having affairs with other men. When he confronted Mark with his suspicions, Mark denied having ever been unfaithful. Yet there was something unsettling about it all.

In time, Dan began pulling away from Mark. He slowly began developing friends and a life of his own that was independent of the relationship. As Mark sensed Dan's pulling away, he became increasingly more attentive and caring. In fact, he went from wanting to have sex once every couple of weeks to almost every night.

This was all deeply confusing to Dan. Was he misreading Mark? Was he the one who had a problem? It seemed every time this had happened before, Dan would respond positively to Mark. It would last a week or two before Mark was back to his old ways. Whenever they talked about it, Mark insisted that Dan was just "too sensitive" and needed counseling. In part, that's why Dan came to see me.

The irony of the situation was that it wasn't Dan who needed the most help. However, Dan was so shaken after living with this behavior for years that he had actually come to believe that he was the one with the problem. When he entered my office, his whole presentation said, "Fix me, I'm broken."

> "Joe was such a game player. The more aloof I was, the more he seemed to want me. When I was available, he wasn't interested. It was like he was more interested in the game than he was in me."
>
> WILLIAM FROM DENVER, CO

The trauma of the ambivalent relationship most often has the effect of creating "relationship helplessness." Relationship helplessness occurs when you believe that no matter what you do and say in a relationship, it won't make a difference. While at first glance it may seem that relationship helplessness is a reaction to a bad relationship, it is much more. In fact, once it starts, it often follows a man through subsequent relationships. It creates a belief that one is helpless to change or positively influence relationships.

Many men who experience relationship helplessness find themselves staying in a bad relationship because they believe that it would be the same in any other relationship. They often give up and settle for something less than satisfying.

Tim and Walter have been together for more than twenty-five years. They met in their mid-twenties and have lived together ever since. Somewhere around ten years into the relationship, Tim grew weary of Walter's ever changing moods and attitudes toward him. One month he was wonderfully pleasant, and another month he seemed to be bored into apathy. Years of riding this relationship roller coaster had worn down Tim's confidence that a relationship could be anything more than this.

Now, fifteen years later, they still sleep in the same bed, but never, ever touch. Tim once remarked that if his foot accidentally touched Walter in the night that both of them would jerk instantly. On the surface they were mildly friendly with each other, but anyone who spent time with them usually saw beneath the surface smiles and felt the palpable tension between them. When I asked Tim why he stays with Walter, he said, "Look around, all relationships end up this way. I'm just glad that we're still together."

Tim had been raised by a single mother who moved around a great deal and had had several different boyfriends when Tim was young. He always yearned for a stable life like his friends had. Every year or so, he had to pick up, move with his mother to another town, and change schools. And that meant leaving one set of friends and being forced to make a whole new set of friends. He had learned his relationship helplessness long before he met

Walter. Walter, it seems, only reinforced what Tim had learned as a child: "I am helpless within relationships."

One gay man said to me, "It would have been easier if he had hit me. At least then there would have been bruises as evidence of the injury. Instead, it was a slow drain on me that eventually destroyed my self-confidence." Ambivalent relationships are as damaging as virtually any form of physical or emotional abuse, sometimes even more so, because on the surface the relationship may seem safe but in reality is anything but. The backs and forths and ups and downs of these relationships slowly tax the gay man's emotional resources.

Chapter 13

THE ROAD TO

CONTENTMENT

Having broken free from the stronghold of shame and the pain of trauma, the gay man begins to build his life—a life of meaning, purpose, and satisfaction. It is the time in life, whether he is twenty-two or seventy-five, that he is truly free to become a unique individual who is able to become his own man, and in the process, find real contentment.

What is it that makes a gay man content? The same things that it takes for anyone else to be content, the only difference being that the gay man isn't free to pursue these things until he reaches stage three. Only then can he clearly and without the distracting influence of shame find contentment.

The three legs that make up the stool of contentment are passion, love, and integrity. Contentment in life rests firmly in the ongoing pursuits of these three things.

PASSION

Passion is a complex and multifaceted code that is implanted into each of us. Breaking that code for all but a few of us becomes a lifelong endeavor. During our early years, it can seem elusive and obscure—so much so that we abandon the pursuit and rest in a complacent and cynical belief that passion simply does not exist for us.

Yet I'm certain that passion exists within each of us. The tragedy of growing up in toxic shame is that we are ill-equipped at best to decipher the code of passion, and the only way we can experience passion is to become a master of the code. To be certain, the discovery of real passion for many gay men is difficult, yet this challenge is not proof of its nonexistence but rather represents the price to be paid for real contentment.

The code of passion is written in the brief but rewarding experiences of joy each of us experiences every day. When we don't know ourselves well or aren't practicing noticing our feelings, the code of passion is hidden from us. Hence, real passion becomes available to the gay man only when he has conquered the toxic shame of his early years. Until then, he may have glimpses and tastes of passion, but the full experience eludes him.

Passion is the repeated experience of joy in doing something. When one discovers passion, it is usually because an activity seems to produce joy each time it is performed. Normally, there is a diminishing return on the joy associated with an activity. Not so when passion is present. The activity produces a surprising and satisfying amount of joy, again and again.

Passion is a meta-emotion—an emotion that is felt only after observing other emotions over time. Passion is present when you observe that the same activity consistently brings you joy.

Since the key to passion is hidden in joy, it's necessary to understand something about the primary emotion of joy. Like all other primary emotions, joy is a behavior within the body. Most commonly, it is described as the feeling of painless lightness within the body.

Joy is fundamentally different than most emotions. Other emotions like shame or sadness, once triggered, can last for twenty minutes or longer. Often these emotions last much longer because we engage in behaviors that cause the chemicals within our bodies that create these emotions to continually be released. For example, when you first feel sad, you have a tendency to think sad thoughts and remember other sad events in your life. This, in turn, causes your sadness to continue. If you continue to dwell on sad memories and thoughts, your overall mood becomes one that is dominated by sadness.

> "The day I quit my job and went back to school to become an architect was the best day of my life. I've never looked back."
>
> CONRAD FROM
> LAS VEGAS, NV

Joy, on the other hand, tends to be a quick and fleeting emotion that can fly past us and go unnoticed. Once it fires within our brains, it may be felt for as little as a few seconds. For instance, the joy at seeing the face of an old friend whom you haven't seen for years; or the joy at hearing that you just received a long-awaited promotion at work—like other emotions, you can cause joy by thinking about or telling the joyous event to other people. All in all, joy tends to be a quick spike in our emotional field, much like an orgasm of the soul. It builds to a quick climax, then just as quickly fades away.

Passion is felt when you notice the joy that is felt frequently when you perform a particular task. If you are not mindful of your emotions in the moment, you don't notice that when you create a new recipe or learn about a rare variety of fish, this elicits passionate feelings. In order for passion to be evoked, joy must first be noticed and felt.

Danny would often bring to his therapy session the most unusual pieces of machinery. They were always small, unusual, and very intricately crafted. He was a machinist at a local metal shop, and he would bring a piece that he thought was interesting.

Danny had suffered from depression for many years prior to coming to therapy, and carefully trained his mind to notice and ruminate on many of the negative things in his life. As is the case with most of us when we are depressed, his mental vision narrowed to a tunnel that filtered out everything but the negative subject in current focus. He had great difficulty imagining himself not being depressed, and stated that he had not felt joy in years. He'd been in several relationships with other men that had been short-lived, mostly because they couldn't tolerate his continually gloomy mood.

What was at the source of Danny's depression wasn't the lack of joy, *it was the lack of noticing joy.* During a period of about a year, Danny had created a dozen or more interesting and functional metal objects that had ever so briefly triggered a spike of joy within him. He loved the experience of creating something that was simultaneously beautiful and useful; he was in many ways a sculptor. The spike of joy often went unnoticed and quickly faded as Danny's mind quickly returned to the negativity and self-invalidation with which it was most comfortable. His memory of these experiences was often occluded by the cloud of depressive emotions that surrounded the experience.

As you can imagine, not being capable of recognizing his own experience of joy, Danny reported that he had never, ever felt passion for anything. He couldn't even imagine what passion was and not surprisingly seriously doubted its existence.

To help Danny be more mindful of joy, he began completing a daily diary of his emotions. Specifically, he was to report in the diary whenever he thought that he might have experienced joy. During the first weeks, Danny reported not feeling any joy. Then, with some prodding on my part, he began reporting very slight instances of joy, usually at having created something interesting at work. Over time, Danny became more mindful of the joy that was actually present in his life. As he noticed it more often, we worked on skills he could use to prolong those moments of joy.

Passion for Danny was clearly centered around his creativity in working with metal. He regularly experienced joy at taking a block of material, combining it with other materials, and carving it into something useful. The more mindful he was of the joy it gave him, the more joy it gave him. Over a period of a year, Danny's depression relented, and for the first time in many years, he began finding some enjoyment in life.

I share Danny's story to point out that most of us aren't mindful of our experience of joy, and therefore ignore passion as well. Because it is a quick and fleeting emotion, it flies past us unnoticed. As a result, we haven't a clue about those things that make us passionate, and it all just seems like psychobabble, happy talk.

The gay man who has spent most of his time in life avoiding shame is also likely to not have discovered his passion in life. He has felt joy—and may be able to recall various joyous experiences, but he has been so preoccupied with avoiding shame that he hasn't developed the skill of noticing joy and prolonging it when it occurs.

The skill of creating and prolonging joy has three parts:

- Make yourself vulnerable to joy.
- Notice when you feel joy.
- Repeat the behaviors that create joy.

The first step in creating joy is to put yourself in the most likely state for joy to occur. For most of us, this state includes having plenty of rest, appropriate nutrition, and a safe environment.

Troy is an artist. His paintings grace the walls of some of the finest hotels and office buildings around the country. To make himself vulnerable to joy (a critical element for him in making his best work), he must be completely rested. Often in the early afternoon, he takes a half-hour nap to ensure that he is adequately rested. Another way he makes himself vulnerable is by listening to his favorite kind of classical music while painting. Being rested, listening to music, and painting in his beloved studio are the factors that make him most vulnerable to feeling joy.

A common problem among people who report that they don't feel joy, or have lost the joy that they once felt, is that they are physically tired and overly stressed. It doesn't matter how much joy you may have experienced while writing if your new job is so stressful that you haven't been able to sleep for days. The writing that once brought you joy is likely in this state of exhaustion to feel like a tedious chore.

To increase your experience of joy, it is helpful to mindfully notice when you are feeling joy. Make it a point to notice your feelings throughout the day. Sometimes using a diary can help with this task. When you feel some joy, even if it is slight, notice what you are doing at the moment and where you are. By recording the behavior and environment in which joy naturally occurs for you, you are better equipped to make yourself feel joy in the future by putting yourself in the same kind of situation again.

A gay man can easily confuse joy with the satisfaction of validation. He may mistake the warm feeling of having other men notice him, perhaps when he works out at the gym or when he enters the room at a party, as joy. Or he may assume that the feeling after the applause of the audience following his performance or the rave review of a critic is joy. While there may be some joy felt in both these situations, there is a difference in experiencing authentic joy and the temporary satisfaction that comes from validation. Joy emerges from inside you and is intrinsically generated. Validation is most often an external event that comes from other people. While external events can trigger the internal experience of joy, it is easy to confuse the two and assume that joy is nothing

> "I got to the point where I just didn't care what my gay friends thought about it. I have wanted to teach elementary school all my life, and now I am finally doing it. I'll never get rich or famous, but it's totally about me."
>
> BILL FROM MINNEAPOLIS, MN

but the experience of validation. Often, the most intense experiences of joy have nothing to do with the validation provided by others.

The distinction between validation and joy is important for the gay man. In the early stages, he was pursuing validation as a defense against shame. Now, in the discovery of his passion, he pursues an activity not because others approve of it, but because it brings him intrinsic joy. Very often, these two activities are quite different.

For Troy the painter, validation comes from having a painting sold to an important collector. Joy, on the other hand, comes to him in the studio when he creates something on canvas that he's never created before. What sells best to collectors is often something that he may have painted many times before. What brings him joy is when he is pushing himself past his limits, reaching deep inside himself, and painting something new and fresh. The fundamental split between what brings Troy validation and what brings him joy is critical. If Troy runs after validation, then he continues to paint those kinds of images that sell best. On the other hand, if Troy seeks joy, he paints what is new and authentic for him—something that may not be as familiar or desirable to collectors. As a gay man learns this important distinction, he unlocks the sequence in the code of passion.

Of course, joy and validation are not always opposed to each other and often occur simultaneously. Eventually, as the gay man structures his life around the pursuit of joy, he becomes surrounded with people who validate his behavior. The key difference, however, is that the pursuit of joy is the primary objective, and validation comes only as a secondary benefit.

One of the three essential components to finding contentment in life is in discovering your passion. To do so, you must first be mindful of the joy you experience, and second, become skillful at maintaining and increasing the experience of joy.

LOVE

Love, like passion, is also a meta-emotion and is the second essential component of finding contentment in life. Also like passion, love is felt only after noticing the ongoing experience of joy. While passion is about feeling joy in an activity, love is about noticing joy in the presence of another person. When the experience of another person regularly stimulates joy within us, we begin to feel we love that person.

The sad truth is that it is difficult to ascertain love when you are driven to avoid shame. Joy is in short supply and much of your attention is consumed with avoiding shame through work, sex, addictions, etc. During stages one and two, what you think is love is often more an appreciation for another person who assists somehow in your quest to avoid shame. He's gorgeous, sexy, successful, talented, or shares your addiction. But relatively few of these things speak to real joy.

When I realized this for myself, I found it deeply disturbing, as do many gay men: the realization that I had never really felt love for another man. Oh, I'd felt it from time to time, a few glimpses here and there, but never consistently for the same man. Real joy comes more from such things as enjoying another's company, connecting emotionally, and common core values. Sure, it helps if he's gorgeous, sexy, talented, or rich, but it isn't the main dish. All of those things we sought in stages one and two had little to do with the simple but powerful experience of joy in the presence of another person.

> "Rick is totally unlike any guy I've dated before. He's really not my type, or so I thought when I met him. He's not conventionally handsome at all, yet I find him extremely sexy now. I've never been with anyone who makes me happier. No matter what is happening, he makes me laugh."
>
> THOMAS FROM
> NEW ORLEANS, LA

When the gay man begins to truly experience love, it is because he is mindful of the subtleties in his partner that bring him joy. A look, a smile, a laugh, a walk, a touch. These consistently bring him joy and pleasure.

Learning to let go of the surface pleasures, and instead being mindful of the consistent joy, leads you down a very different path in seeking a partner. No longer are you looking for a man who fits your predefined "features" list, but rather you are wanting to experience a man who stirs an unspeakable happiness within you. He may not be young, gorgeous, muscled, or rich. The truth is, all this becomes irrelevant. He brings you real joy, and you to him, and that's all that matters.

If you're brave, the next time you say you love someone in your life, ask yourself: Does this person bring me joy? If you answer honestly, the answer will at times surprise—maybe even shock—you. Not until you are mindful of your authentic experience of joy are you truly able to feel love. Anything less isn't love.

INTEGRITY

The last of the three essential components of contentment is integrity. Integrity really cuts to the core of the struggle of the gay man, meaning *integrate all parts of oneself,* or more formally, *the state of being undivided.* For the gay man, it means the absence of hiding parts of yourself, no longer splitting, and allowing all parts of yourself to be known. Since this is the principal journey of the gay man as he moves from shame to authenticity, the attainment of integrity represents a crowning achievement.

Even after the gay man has entered stage three, integrity can sometimes be difficult to maintain. So practiced are we at hiding unpleasant truths, no matter how small or large, we easily slip back into old, familiar habits.

Integrity becomes a mindful practice for the gay man who chooses to maintain it. He cannot rely on the momentum of his past nor his own intentions to make integrity a regular part of his life. He must consciously attend to all the ways in which he can maintain integrity.

Rico was a real estate agent in a small but wealthy ski resort town. He and his partner had lived in the town for many years and had ridden the wave of prosperity as the town's real estate had boomed into the stratosphere. Now normal residents of this otherwise rural town included movie stars, famous authors, and a very well-known talk show host.

Rico's partner was some twenty years older than he, and had begun to look his age as he entered his sixties. Rico, on the other hand, was quite young-looking and very handsome. Rico was committed to his relationship, although he enjoyed toying with some of his gay male out-of-town clients whom he would chauffeur around town, from house to house, all the while flirting and flashing his incredible smile. On not a few occasions, Rico would successfully close a real estate deal having the client infatuated with him because he failed to mention that he wasn't really available. At other times, he would withhold this information just long enough during the first meeting to see if he could catch the eye of his client, and then casually mention something about his boyfriend. It was a bit of an unconscious game with Rico, intended to elicit confirmation that he was still attractive to other men.

Mindful integrity requires that the gay man monitor all the ways in which he may be hiding himself, no matter how insignificant, and taking steps to correct them. As in the case of Rico, integrity calls for complete honesty even in what Rico commonly omitted from his initial relationship with his clients.

Being clear and straightforward about who we are, what we want from others, and our intentions is the cornerstone of integrity.

Even at times when it seems smart to not be completely honest or forthcoming, integrity necessitates that we act against this urge. Not only does this action build our own sense of self-worth (i.e., "who I am is worth presenting to the world"), it also builds fulfilling and emotionally healthy relationships. For Rico, he had noticed that many of his relationships in town were somewhat superficial and lacked the fundamental "connectedness" that he wanted. Furthermore, he realized that he had acquired the reputation of being a player and a tease, and other gay men seemed to hold him at a distance.

The learning and practice of passion, love, and integrity is what creates meaningful contentment in our lives. Once we have shed the shackles of shame, and seek to create a life worth living, these three become the ultimate goals of our lives.

Chapter 14

SKILLS FOR LIVING

AN AUTHENTIC LIFE

For well over a hundred years, most major schools of thought in psychotherapy were based on one rather questionable assumption: *insight into childhood experiences creates changes in adult behavior.* If you had seen a psychotherapist in the 1940s, you might have entered a wood-paneled office that was lined with books and archetypal artifacts that were thought to have deeper meaning in your unconscious mind. The therapist might have smoked during the session (an odd artifact of the therapeutic culture of the time), and through that smoky haze, the two of you would have strolled down the dark corridors of your childhood experience, looking for unresolved conflicts that could be raised into conscious awareness. The holy grail of each session was to attain "insight," or an intellectual awareness of deeper-seated emotional conflicts. This basic model of psychotherapy has largely predominated the field until the present day, despite mounting evidence that while attaining insight into one's childhood can be immensely satisfying and comforting, it is not sufficient to bring about a change in behavior. For example, the alcoholic patient

might explore his history of childhood emotional abuse and neglect, and still leave each session drinking heavily, destroying his
relationships and career, and ultimately committing a slow suicide. Insight into his past experiences may explain why he has
come to use alcohol as his primary coping mechanism, but it does
not offer him a way to change. Hence, in the case of the alcoholic,
Alcoholics Anonymous (AA) emerged, offering direct advice on
what behaviors must be learned and practiced if one is to stop a
dependency on alcohol and live a fulfilling life. What AA offered
were "skills"—simple behaviors that could be practiced repeatedly until they became part of one's natural behavioral repertoire.
AA offered no deep insight into childhood experience but rather
a clear focus on what the alcoholic can do right now—one day at
a time—to change his or her life.

As it turns out, most of the research into psychotherapy estab-
lishes that AA got it right. Significant life change is all about
learning and practicing skills until those new behaviors become
a natural part of your life. There have been several highly effective therapies that developed out of this research, including cognitive behavioral therapy, dialectical behavior therapy, and acceptance and commitment therapy, just to name a few. All of
these therapies share one principle in common: *meaningful life
change comes from mindful practice.*

No doubt you have experienced this in other areas of your life.
If you want to change your body, you might have hired a trainer
and regularly met with him or her at a gym so that you could
learn the correct exercises and consistently practice what you
have learned to create the body you want. If you have ever
learned to play a musical instrument, picked up a foreign language, or learned a new sport, you did it through consistent
practice of a skill—not by simply acquiring insight into the ac-

tivity. It makes no sense to say, for example, that you don't need to take a spinning class because you already understand what spinning is about. The real change comes from getting on the spinning bicycle and riding it for an entire class.

This chapter is a carefully collected list of skills that have been developed over decades of hard work—most of which were taught to me by my clients who embraced their own struggle for authenticity. In compiling this list, I've selected only those skills that are essential and effective in bringing positive change into our lives as gay men. Think of this as a shortcut through years—really decades—of therapy.

As you read over these skills, you will see the wisdom inherent in them. However, reading is not the point. This chapter is a short list of "must do's"—behaviors, not insights; actions, not ideas—that is, necessary choices that must be made if contentment is to be found. It is daily practice, not contemplation, that creates the life you want.

Of everything contained in this book, this chapter is the most important. Regardless of the stage you are in, the regular and consistent practice of these skills will bring you fully and consistently into stage three authenticity. I often say that the journey from the head to the heart is taken with your feet—meaning that the only way to really integrate insights into your life is by behaving differently. Consistent and continuous practice is the magic that makes the real difference in our lives.

One way in which gay men have found support in living these skills is by meeting once a week in a group to discuss and hold one another accountable for living "skillfully." This can be a wonderful and life-changing experience, especially when facilitated by a trained therapist who can assist the group in staying on track with the skills, and not getting lost in the "story" we tell

ourselves to justify less than skillful behavior. For more information on forming a *Velvet Rage* group and for helpful tools, visit
www.alandowns.com.

At the end of this chapter is a summary chart of the skills with
a brief description of each skill. Many of the gay men that I work
with have found it helpful to make a copy of this chart and keep
it handy, so they can review it regularly as a reminder of the man
they wish to become and the skills they would like to incorporate
more often in their lives.

LIFE CHOICES

Every moment of every day, every breath you take presents an
opportunity to choose a life of contentment and joy. Here, in the
small decisions, is where you make choices that ultimately make
a big difference in your life. It's easy to imagine that the big decisions, things like changing a job or ending a relationship, make
the biggest difference in my life, but this is not so. Most often
when I make big changes, I quickly discover that I re-create the
same mess I was trying to escape before I made the change. Big
moves create upheaval and a distraction from whatever may be
causing me distress, but inevitably the same old stuff comes back
around with a different costume.

John was determined that Los Angeles was the worst possible
place to be middle-aged and single. "All the WeHo guys are tens
who are looking for elevens!" he exclaimed to me during one session, referring to the ten-point rating system used on popular reality contests. John had a fairly successful career as a marketing
executive for a company that owned parking lots. While not a terribly sexy industry, the company had done extraordinarily well

throughout John's career, and he had benefited such that he was able to retire in his late forties with a decent retirement stashed away if he was careful with his spending. John had been in a long-term relationship with another man that had lasted a decade and a half, and he had been single, quite unhappily, for the past four years. His therapy was often a recounting of the various dates and online dating encounters he would have with other gay men. With his fiftieth year just around the corner, John decided that he needed to make a big change—that would be the only way he would find a partner. He sold his home in Los Angeles, said good-bye to lifelong close friends, and moved to Savannah, Georgia, where he had grown up. Thinking a simpler life in a small town would facilitate meeting a man who was more down-to-earth than the West Hollywood crowd he had tried unsuccessfully to date, he created a life in Savannah in hopes of a fresh new start.

That was the last I heard from John until, quite to my surprise, I ran into him on the street during a visit to Key West some two years later. Still single, bored with life in a small town, and full of the same complaints about gay men (only now it was those "Southern queens"), he was already planning to move to Atlanta, where he imagined the selection of single gay men was more plentiful. "After all, it's a numbers game."

John had enacted the classic "geographic"—moving to another geographic location thinking that will change his life for the better. Unfortunately for John, he was unwilling to see that his problems in dating stemmed more from his inability to be vulnerable with almost anyone, other than his therapist—and only then after much encouragement and support. He had previously been in a relationship that had been somewhat emotionally cold—almost businesslike—and that reinforced in him a tendency to hide his deepest feelings and insecurities from others.

We all know intellectually that changing our circumstances doesn't change us on the inside, and yet we often cling to the fantasy that the big change—a new job, making a lot of money, a new boyfriend, or a new city—will be just the ticket. It rarely is.

Every day, every decision we make presents us with the opportunity to choose differently. It is here, in the daily practice of choosing contentment over others' approval, valuing inner peace above all, and living by our values instead of our feelings, that we change for the better.

The man I would become

Skill: When faced with an important life decision, ask yourself: "What would the man I wish to become do in this situation?" Take a moment and listen carefully to what your heart tells you, and after careful consideration, act on it.

Background: The secret to creating a content and fulfilled life is by living according to your most treasured values. Often our values are closely held—so closely that it can be sometimes difficult to know them directly. By picturing the man you want to become—your ideal "you"—you can access those most treasured values as manifested in this image.

What gets in the way of using this skill is not in knowing what the man we would like to become would do; rather, it is in the willingness to act on what we know. Most often caught up in the emotion of the moment or wanting a quick escape from our current pain, we choose not to act on what we know is in our highest and best interest.

None us gets it right all the time, and each of us in our own way becomes willfully determined to act against what we know is in our best interest. We aspire to always be willing, but in those moments when that's not possible, we do ourselves a service by at least being mindful that we have consciously made a choice that isn't consistent with our own values. Judgment, shame, and self-deprecation rarely help in these moments. Just by noticing your own willfulness, you'll begin to change in a positive direction.

Inner peace above all else

Skill: When trying to decide between two or more options in life, honestly assess which option is most likely to contribute to your own inner peace. Choose the option that holds the greatest promise of bringing you peace in the long term.

Background: When the noise of conflicting feelings, life pressures, and such reaches a crescendo in our minds, it is easy to lose our perspective on what is important. We can convince ourselves that choices that promise success, money, love, and popularity are in our best interest, but is that same choice likely to increase our experience of inner peace? At the end of it all, what matters most is being at peace with ourselves, and nothing more. Not accomplishments, possessions, relationships, money, or fame. So, no matter what you think you might gain from a particular decision, if it doesn't ultimately contribute to your attainment of inner peace, it isn't worth it.

Nowhere is this skill more valuable than in your choice of life partners. We've been taught to choose the partner that ignites our fire and makes us feel the heat of love and attraction—sometimes at the expense of many other key relationship elements; if that relationship doesn't contribute to your own sense of peace and contentment, the cost is just too high.

My client Alex is a great example here. Alex called my assistant and asked to see me at the first available opening. My assistant, who is very adept at sensing serious distress, asked Alex if he was suicidal, and he replied that he was seriously thinking about killing himself but wouldn't likely act on it. During our first session, the story flowed out of Alex like a rushing river. He had led a quiet life as a junior high school history teacher until he met Craig. Craig was an incredibly hot-looking man who was completely taken with Alex. During the first year of their relationship things went mostly smoothly, but Craig seemed to grow increasingly unsatisfied in the relationship even though his words were that he was happy with Alex. When Craig and Alex went out on the weekends, Craig began expressing an interest in picking up other men for the two of them to have sex with. Alex, not really interested in the idea of three-ways, went along, hoping it would make Craig happy. As time went on, Craig began to occasionally use crystal meth on weekends and would cruise the local park to find men to bring home for Alex and Craig to have sex with. Eventually, Craig began spending most of his free time online searching for men, and one night when they were out at a bar, Craig overdosed on GHB and had to be rushed to the emergency room. By the time Alex and Craig hit the three-year mark, word had spread around town about the couple, and even fellow teachers at Alex's school had heard some of the stories. Two weeks prior to Alex coming in to see me, Craig was arrested for having sexual relations with a minor. Because he had done this while living in Alex's home, Alex had been placed on leave from his teaching job until there could be a complete investigation. Now Alex faced losing his employment, possibly ending his career, and dealing with a boyfriend who clearly had a serious drug-infused sex addiction.

Alex's story isn't unique. The signs of Craig's sexual craziness and tendency toward addiction had been present from the beginning, but Alex was swept off his feet by how attracted he was to Craig. Even in the beginning, Alex had some idea that a life with Craig wouldn't likely be easy, but he was so damn good-looking. Alex, like so many of us have done, buried his head in the sand and hoped for the best.

Whether it is who you date, the job you choose, or the friends with whom you spend time, always ask yourself if the choice is likely to contribute to your own inner peace. If the honest answer is "no," then take a hard look at why you are wanting to make a choice that isn't in your ultimate best interest. Sometimes we do it to escape the pain or boredom of our current circumstances, sometimes out of loneliness, and still at other times because we are hungry for validation. All of these are legitimate needs that are better addressed directly, rather than acquired at the cost of our own contentment.

Never react while feeling an intense emotion

Skill: When feeling an intense emotion, ALWAYS delay taking action until after the emotion has subsided. Rarely do we make the best choices when under the influence of intense emotion, and worse, it is at those moments that we are often convinced that we are absolutely right and must take action immediately. Notice the feeling and immediately take whatever steps you can to allow the emotion to subside before acting. Write the e-mail, but save it rather than send it. Don't pick up the phone. Refuse to make the purchase. Walk away from the conversation. Do nothing until the emotion has diminished.

Background: The key to this skill is twofold. First, notice that you are feeling an emotion. Second, consider whether or not it is effective for you to act on that emotion. Is it really effective to tell off your boss because he criticized you in public? Is it effective for you to spend the night at a friend's house every time your lover complains about something you've done? There's nothing wrong or inappropriate with feeling the emotions of anger or shame in these two examples. However, acting on these emotions in the moment isn't really helpful. It certainly doesn't help the situation improve, and worse still, it is likely to cause you to feel more of this emotion in the future.

An important point to understand is that there is a big difference between *feeling* an emotion and *acting* on it. You are capable of feeling a wide range of intense emotions, but just because you feel them doesn't mean you are helpless and must immediately take the bull by the horns. That's like saying the murderer couldn't help his actions because he was enraged, or the embezzler isn't responsible for stealing because he feared at the time for his own financial well-being. Emotions in healthy, functioning, nonpsychotic individuals are not valid rationalizations for actions. Emotions inform us but control us only if we allow them to.

Creating the "contemplative moment" between feeling and action is an important practice for authenticity. Feelings in the moment aren't always representative of what we consistently feel over time, so expressing these impulsive feelings can communicate inaccuracies about ourselves. Telling your lover that you haven't enjoyed sex with him because lately he seems less interested in sex is likely inaccurate and inauthentic. Or telling your new boyfriend that you've known only for a few hours that you love him is equally inauthentic. Acting on an emotional urge isn't necessarily honest, authentic, or effective. In fact, it will most likely do harm.

Intense emotions create a full-body response, much in the same way that alcohol or mood-altering substances work. Your reaction time, perception, judgment, and sensitivity to your environment are all affected by the emotion. One of the most notable effects of a strong emotion is that it limits your focus and memory to those things to which the emotion is attached. When you are angry with a friend, in that moment, what occupies most of your attention are the circumstances that elicited the anger. It is harder to recall the times when your friend was kind or helpful, for example.

It's never a good idea to make decisions when in an altered state. When you are under the influence of a strong emotion, it has two notable properties: (1) the emotion screams in your brain, and (2) it has a sense of urgency seemingly saying "do it now!" How many times have you made a phone call or sent an e-mail when feeling something intensely, only to regret it the next day after the emotion has subsided?

Contentment over approval

Skill: Choose those investments in life that contribute to your sense of feeling contentment, rather than those investments of your time and energy that promise to earn you the acceptance or approval of others.

Background: Since we were young boys, most of us were heavily focused on winning the acceptance of others to compensate for that inner feeling of being unacceptable, perhaps even unlovable. As men, we can continue this pattern by choosing careers, partners, and friends based on what we imagine will make us more acceptable to others rather than those things that are intrinsically rewarding to us. Putting the effects of shame behind you and getting your life back on track to authenticity demands that you examine all of your emotional investments for their "intrinsic" value to bring you contentment versus their "extrinsic" value to bring you acceptance and the approval of others. Only those that increase and support your contentment will ultimately bring you joy and fulfillment; all others will drain you of energy and time that could be spent doing something that brings a far more meaningful return.

Jim is an artist who makes a decent living selling his paintings in local galleries. He's not getting rich, by any stretch, but he pays his bills and loves the fact that this time is his own and he doesn't have to report to a boss. On several occasions, he has had the opportunity to take other jobs, particularly in the field of graphic and website design. These jobs pay better than what he can make from his art but would require that he work on projects that are assigned as opposed to working on his own art. He's often been tempted to take a job so he could have money to do some of the extras, like take a great vacation, fix up his house, or drive a nicer car.

It's not that there's anything innately wrong with Jim taking a job, and at some point it might even be wise. However, the right job for Jim has to offer him the ability to express his artistic talents in a way that brings him contentment rather than just a paycheck. While the latter might make him feel more accepted and successful, in the long run it's likely to make him unhappy and dissatisfied with his life.

The most important thing to remember about this skill is that *contentment is created when your behavior is consistent with your values.* When you act in ways that are consistent with the core of who you are, even when your actions aren't approved by others, you increase your overall contentment. Happiness, success, money, relationships, and even the approval of others will come and go in your life, but what is ultimately satisfying is feeling content—regardless of these other more transitory highs and lows. Making the decision to act according to your core values rather than what brings approval from others ultimately makes you more content in life.

INCREASING POSITIVE EMOTIONS

The skills in this section are particularly effective at helping to contain and reduce the experience of negative emotions and increase your positive experience of life. Finding contentment and inner peace is almost entirely dependent on our ability to limit the negative emotions and interpretations of life. Learning the practice of containing the negative, and actively employing the willingness to do so, is the secret to a happy life.

Without realizing it, you may already practice the following skills. But by bringing these skills into awareness and initiating focused practice, you increase your daily experience of joy and overall satisfaction with life. While none of these skills is particularly unique to gay men, I find that many of us either don't use these skills or don't practice them regularly.

Accept reality on reality's terms

Skill: When life doesn't turn out the way you want, stop insisting that it not be so. This is a skill that is rarely practiced once and accomplished successfully; rather, it requires repeated use until you finally relinquish the demand that life be something different than what it is.

Background: In Alcoholics Anonymous, most meetings include the recitation of the serenity prayer, which reads: "God, grant me the serenity to accept the things I cannot change, courage to change the things I can, and wisdom to know the difference." In this ancient prayer is contained the essence of the acceptance skill—learning to accept those things that cannot be changed.

Many years ago, I attended a professional training workshop in which the speaker made the statement that "everything is perfectly as it should be" to illustrate the essence of the skill of acceptance. I'll never forget the uproar that followed that comment, as it seemed that everyone in the room disagreed with the speaker. For years I struggled with this statement, until I reached the point of understanding that what "should be" is always "what is." In other words, the speaker was stating that there really are no "should's" in the world, only what is. The "shoulds" are fantasies, large and small, and are not reality—they do not exist.

Most often when we experience distress in life it's because we consistently and rigidly refuse to accept reality, or "what is," and demand that it be something different. You refuse to accept that your partner is not responsible with money, no matter how much you insist that he be so. Or you refuse to accept the body you were born with and keep trying to change it, hide it, or create the illusion that it is different from what it is.

If you're like me, you're probably thinking, "Yes, but isn't there something to be said for being dissatisfied with the status quo and reaching for something higher?" This is the dialectic (two seemingly opposing truths that don't necessarily cancel one another out) that is at the heart of this skill. In short, this skill requires we first accept everything about reality before we even consider making a change. For example, you must accept that your partner does not naturally have the skills to manage money and may even have a resistance to learning such skills. Is it possible, in some future reality, that he will acquire these skills? Perhaps, but the present moment requires that you accept where he is, for only then will you be able to see the opportunities to truly help him to acquire the skills, and perhaps the desire, to manage money more effectively.

Keith absolutely dreads going to work. More to the point, he hates his boss. He's been passed over for a promotion on at least three occasions, and his boss consistently takes personal credit for Keith's work. Every time this happens, Keith goes into a quiet rage—which he sometimes takes out at home on his partner. Keith's boss has been something of a cut-throat, self-centered person since Keith first took the job. His behavior isn't fair and clearly hurts Keith's chances of getting a promotion and making more money; nonetheless, this is who he is. Keith's refusal to accept that his boss behaves badly causes Keith great distress every time his boss does something to undercut him. If Keith truly accepted his boss for who he is, his anger would lessen. The boss's behavior isn't right, and nobody expects Keith to like it, but it is the reality of his boss.

Keith often would proclaim things like "but he shouldn't take credit for my work" or "I deserve the promotion—I've earned it." Whenever life begins to feel blatantly unfair, ask yourself if there's something you need to accept. Persistent and troubling feelings of unfairness are often based on one's unwillingness to accept some aspect of reality. Likewise, when something seems absolutely unbearable (i.e., "I can't take it"), that is also most often a sign that we are refusing to accept some aspect of reality.

It is extremely helpful to remember that acceptance is not approval. Very often, those things that we must accept in life are also those things we do not like, and perhaps even despise. You likely would not choose to be HIV-positive and may even despise what that virus has done to our community and world, but if you test positive for the HIV antibody, you must accept that you are HIV-positive. To consistently refuse to accept this keeps you in continuous, excessive, and unnecessary suffering.

When Joe found out he was HIV-positive, he was devastated. He made an appointment with one of the best HIV doctors in Los Angeles, but did so under an assumed name and made the appointment at a time when he figured there wouldn't be many other men in the waiting room. Six months later, Joe came to therapy seeking help with a new relationship. He'd finally met the man of his dreams, and the only problem was that he hadn't revealed his HIV status to his boyfriend. While he was insistent that they practice only safe sex, he was terrified that his boyfriend would have a problem with his HIV status and might even break off the relationship because of it. And if he didn't have a problem with Joe being HIV-positive, he would most surely have a problem with not being told of it. Joe's refusal to truly and fully accept his HIV status prevented him from being completely honest about it from the beginning of the relationship. For if Joe had fully accepted his status, he would be quite clear that no matter how great the boyfriend might be, the relationship hasn't much of a chance unless he reveals his status— since it isn't likely to change until there is an effective vaccine. Perhaps you can remember how much distress you felt when you dated a man prior to being out of the closet. Once you fully accepted that you were gay and were honest about it with the important people in your life, much of that distress disappeared.

One thing, one person, one conversation in the moment

Skill: Make it your goal to do only one thing in each moment. It's almost impossible to be fully present for the person who sits in front of you, to experience the joy of a wonderful meal, or even to get the most out of an exercise workout when your mind is jumping between two or more things. You miss the satisfaction and joy of the present moment when you aren't focused on it or when you treat the moment as simply a way to get to the next one.

Background: After spending an evening at a cocktail party in Beverly Hills, a friend explained the concept of "glistening" to me. Glistening happens when a gay man pretends to be listening to you but is really looking over your shoulder to see if there is someone else he should be talking to or is listening to someone else's conversation. When my friend told me about glistening, I laughed, as I thought about all the many conversations I've had at various events with gay men where this is exactly what was happening. And, of course, it forced me to consider how many times I've done the very same thing.

Whenever life starts piling up, and the stress mounts, it is extraordinarily helpful to take some time and make a short list of the things that are really important. Then take that list and do one thing at a time to completion until the list is complete. It's amazing how powerful this skill is in containing the stress and anxiety that often accompanies feeling overwhelmed.

One of the things that is said about the power of Bill Clinton as a politician was his ability to make you feel as if you were the only person in the room. Somewhere along the way, Bill mastered the skill of "one person, one conversation." This skill not only helps to manage your own emotions but also is very powerful in building relationships with others.

It is possible to actually miss the experience of your life by being too distracted with multitasking. You create so much busyness and activity that you fail to truly engage with what is present. For example, I can remember many times when I was throwing a dinner party or a special event and was so involved in making all the details happen that I wasn't able to really experience the joy of the event. Life is just like this—many times we are so caught up in all the busyness that we aren't able to be present for the experience.

This skill is absolutely essential if we are to experience the emotion of joy. Of all the emotions, joy is the one that requires that you be fully present in the moment. When you aren't fully present, you can't feel joy.

Take a nonjudgmental stance whenever possible

Skill: Actively resist the temptation to place everything in your life on a "good-bad continuum." Instead of evaluating your experience according to your expectations, focus your efforts on being present for what is, rather than what you wish would be.

Background: "But we make judgments every day. We'd be totally screwed if we weren't making careful decisions about other people. I just don't get it." Justin slumped back into the chair across from me. I knew what he was struggling with, and I had done my best to explain it to him, but sadly, I was failing miserably.

Justin had an aura of arrogance around him. I felt it almost immediately when he entered my office for the first time. His facial expressions and tone of voice communicated volumes. He seemed to say, "I really don't need therapy . . . and I certainly am not one of your usual clients." Within an hour of meeting him I found myself struggling with my own feelings of dislike and judgment about him. When he left my office after that first session, I secretly hoped he wouldn't return.

But he did. And during our work together, I first had to place my own feelings in perspective. Did I really know anything about this man? Was he intentionally putting forth this cynical arrogance, or was it mere habit?

As it turns out, Justin had been raised by two brilliant parents, both of whom had earned PhDs in their respective fields, and nothing he could do ever impressed them. It was always just not good enough, or he was reminded that he could have done better if he had tried harder. His arrogance as an adult had been his only way of coping in such an invalidating environment as a child. Not only was he forced to demand respect from others, he also learned to be highly critical of everyone around him.

As you might imagine, Justin didn't have many close friends. And the friends he did have kept him at a safe distance. Undoubtedly they enjoyed his biting sense of cynical humor and discriminating tastes, but they likely also feared that it was just a matter of time before he turned his judgments on them and skewered them with his words as he had so many others. Justin was good in small doses, but too much of him felt very dangerous.

The lesson that Justin was forced to learn in his late thirties is a lesson that we must all wrestle with at some point: the failure to accept others for who they are only serves to increase your own distress (it certainly doesn't change the reality of who the other person is). The biting, cynical humor may earn laughs all around, but it also sends a powerful message that you are dangerous to be around.

Those of us who are most intolerant and judgmental of others' faults are inevitably even judgmental about ourselves. In private, we see ourselves as flawed and shameful. The expression of judgment upon others is nothing less than what we deliver to ourselves.

Mindfully taking a nonjudgmental stance is the practice of suspending judgment until all the data are in. Most often when we are judgmental, we have reached a premature conclusion about someone else. We have eagerly ascribed the failures we observed to imagined character flaws. Sometimes we are correct, but many times we are not. A nonjudgmental stance gives the other person space to be human and flawed.

Because gay men grow up struggling with such intense toxic shame, as adults we can be highly judgmental of ourselves and others. We see critical flaws in ourselves, and we are equally harsh in our assessments of others. Taking a nonjudgmental stance means that you have first dealt with your own shame and have now intentionally modified the long-standing habit of pointing out the perceived flaws in others.

How many relationships have you experienced where every conversation eventually gets around to judging someone else's flaws or blaming someone else for your problems? When you get down to it, a surprising number of relationships among gay men are just this. The only common ground the two men share is complaints, cynicism, and blame.

The more critical you are of others, the more difficult it is for you to reveal your true self to the world around you. When you have not allowed others to be less than perfect, does it not only follow that you cannot be less than perfect? And since you know you aren't perfect, how can you possibly reveal yourself? Creating an environment for authenticity requires that we give others the space to be authentic as well. We intuitively know that we can't require something of others that we haven't required of ourselves.

Just remember: even when you're right, you are wrong when you are judgmental toward yourself or others.

Obsessing about pain creates more pain

Skill: When feeling distressing emotions, make a conscious effort to let the pain subside. Continuously replaying painful memories, talking about your pain with others, or exposing yourself to situations that keep the memories active only function to keep you in distress. Deliberately and intentionally take action that distracts you from continuing to reinjure yourself with painful thoughts or memories.

Background: Over the first hundred years of psychology, much of the field was influenced by the psychodynamic "expressive" therapies. To grossly oversimplify, these therapies recommended that one express emotions in order to "get them out" and to relieve the "psychological pressure." In the new millennium of science, things have changed dramatically. Many psychological researchers have established that the expression of an emotion acts as a reinforcer of the emotion, causing it to be more likely to be felt again in the future.

For example, if you are feeling depressed, and you talk about your depression with your friend, expressing all of your self-doubts, hopelessness, and sadness, you are more likely to continue to feel depressed. If, however, your friend stops you from ruminating about your depression and convinces you to go to the movies with him, you are more likely to feel even a little better afterward. Acting on the expressive emotions by talking at length about them usually serves to strengthen those feelings, not lessen them as previously thought. Distracting yourself with a movie prevents you from acting on the depressive emotions, and so they are more likely to fade away.

Obviously, complicated and enduring emotional states like depression or chronic anxiety are far more difficult to relieve than by just going to a movie, but the theory is the same. The more you act on an emotion, the more of that emotion you are likely to feel in the future.

This skill is both extremely important and difficult to practice. When you feel a strong emotion, you naturally want to express it. But unfortunately, the continued expression of an emotion only serves to make the emotion stronger and more likely to happen again in the future; and when the emotion is painful, the act of prolonged expression only increases the experience of your pain.

When you are experiencing a distressing emotion, the most effective course of action is to engage in something that elicits an equally strong, opposite emotion. This, in turn, will prevent you from wallowing in the distress as your mind becomes occupied with the new emotion. For example, if you are feeling lonely after the breakup of a relationship, spend time with close friends talking about their lives. Or start planning a party or a vacation. Do something (with the emphasis on the "do" and not the "thinking" or "obsessing") that elicits a different feeling, and your mind will naturally loosen its grip on the previous distress. Often, this skill must be practiced repeatedly as our minds are accustomed to going back and picking up an old worry or distressing emotion. Just keep engaging in activities that will force the distress to naturally diminish.

Walk your way out of distress

Skill: When feeling uncomfortable emotions like sadness, fear, or anger, deliberately engage in a *behavior* that "changes the channel." In these moments, arguing with yourself or trying to think your way back to serenity isn't feasible—only engaging in behavior (i.e., contrary action) will make the difference.

Background: Jerry's partner, Don, did it again. They were out at a restaurant with friends when Don made a joke about Jerry's lack of good taste in clothes. Jerry was livid—this wasn't the first time Don had done this; in fact, Jerry had asked Don countless times before to not use him as the brunt of his brilliant but cutting humor. In moments like these, Jerry usually shuts down and becomes sullenly quiet. It's not so much about punishing Don as it is that he has a hard time thinking about anything other than what just happened and how angry he is. Don plows on through the evening, laughing and joking, seemingly oblivious to Jerry's distress. It's usually not until the couple is in private that Jerry confronts Don about his behavior, Don apologizes, and over the course of several hours, Jerry slowly returns to being himself again.

In moments of distress like Jerry was experiencing, trying to play "mind tricks" by forcing yourself to think of something else or to challenge the validity of what you feel isn't very effective—in fact, it usually makes things worse. The most effective thing you can do in those moments is to engage in a behavior that helps to both distract and soothe you. For instance, Jerry could have taken a walk to the restroom, stepped outside to make a phone call, or immediately started a conversation with someone else at the dinner table. "Walking" away from distress means simply that you must use your behavior to change the way you are feeling and to reduce the distress. Once you get the distressing feelings down, you can then consider more effective options for getting what you want—as opposed to blowing up or overreacting. Remember, rarely when feeling intense emotions do you act in your own best interest.

Respect your body

Skill: Honor your body as you would a precious possession. Refuse to place your body in deliberate jeopardy. Adore your body, for it is the only one you will ever have.

Background: "Does my butt look big in these jeans?" is a question that will send just about any gay man running for safety. We all know that there is only one acceptable answer to that question, and anyone who is asking such a question is probably a bit too big for those Lucky Dungarees.

Fat. Muscles. Penis size. These are the body obsessions of many gay men. Countless hours at the gym are invested in achieving the perfect arms, chest, butt, and legs. Body fat is considered a medical disability, and having a small penis is a plain and simple tragedy.

The body image issues of gay men are wildly out of control. We have objectified the male physique to the point that many feel that they aren't worthy of a relationship with another man unless they have at least tried to improve their bodies. We see sex as something of a beauty pageant and less an intimate connection of lovemaking. In short, it's all about the body.

Many gay men that I work with see their bodies through the lens of future attainments. By this I mean that they tolerate their current body because they hold the belief that in a few months or years, it will be much improved. "I need to lose this layer of body fat so my abs will show." "When summer comes, I will be in top shape for the beach." They never actually accept their body as it is in the present moment.

Dark, hairy men wish that they were blond and smooth. Short, stocky guys wish that they were linebacker-sized. Tall, thin men work to achieve a more rounded, muscular look. No matter what the body type, there's always some other image to aspire to.

Accepting your body as it is may seem like the beginning of the long slide into pot bellies and dimpled thighs. After all, if you don't force yourself to stay on top of it, isn't the natural flow of life toward entropy?

Accepting your body in the present moment isn't about not having fitness goals. It's about loving who you are and how you look right now, no matter what changes you might make in the future. It's about knowing that making changes in your body is a worthwhile hobby, but it isn't going to make you more desirable or loveable.

Sure, a really hot, chiseled body will get you noticed and probably even a date or two. But at the end of the day, it isn't part of the equation of an emotionally satisfying relationship. Once your suitors have taken in the image of your bulging body parts, it all becomes something like wallpaper, taken for granted with each encounter. Look around and notice that gay men with amazing bodies don't have more successful relationships than other gay men. In fact, from where I sit, it seems as if they have far fewer.

Eric was a gorgeous trainer at the gym. This guy had it all—a handsome, boyish face, a massive smooth chest, and a generously endowed crotch. When I would run on the treadmill, I'd notice newcomers to the gym as they walked in the door. It was only a matter of seconds before they saw Eric and did a double take. He was really that stunning.

What was even more amazing about Eric was that unless he was in tip-top shape, having just pumped his muscles to their fullest, he felt embarrassed. He scheduled his personal workouts in the evenings to ensure that he looked his best when he later went out on the town. If he ever allowed himself to indulge too much and gained a pound or two, he retreated to his apartment after work and hid out until he had lost the extra weight.

You've got to realize that even on a bad day, Eric was as close to an Adonis as a man can be. Yet he could never really see it. He was always focused on how he needed to work on his calf muscles or gain more definition in his abdomen—there was always something about himself that he couldn't accept and needed to change.

Eric may seem a bit freakish, but anyone who has hung out around a gay men's gym knows that he is by no means alone. And while he may be an extreme case, Eric illustrates a problem that plagues large numbers of gay men: a persistent inability to accept their bodies.

The nonacceptance of your body is yet one more expression of the internal shame. The apparent motive for body building is to achieve a beautiful physique; however, the underlying motive is to relieve shame. It's all about making yourself more acceptable and less flawed, and in short, less shameful.

In terms of cultivating authenticity, it is critical to come to terms with your body. It may not be perfect, but it is who you are in the present moment. It represents all the excesses and exercise, displaying the evidence for all to see. Your body doesn't lie.

Not only is body acceptance an important part of authenticity, it is also an important factor in intimate relationships. When you focus on your body and place undue importance on your looks, you naturally attract and gravitate to others who do the same. The most common result of this is relationships that are relatively shallow and short-lived.

Eric's relationships were always with men who were equally stunning. It was plain to see that he rarely took interest in another gay man unless that man was equally muscled and gorgeous. Eric's photo album of ex-boyfriends looked like the roster of a modeling agency.

The problem with Eric's relationships, however, was that they were usually intense and short-lived. It was only a matter of time before he or his boyfriend-of-the-moment would become bored with the other's body image and would decide to move on to someone else. By the time I met Eric, he was already deep into relationship hopelessness, believing that the best kind of relationship was a one-night stand with no obligations.

Of course, a great body doesn't doom you to bad relationships. It does, however, send a very subtle message to others: "physique is very important to me—maybe even the most important thing—so if you want to be with me, you better have something to offer." Other men who may be incredibly interesting and emotionally compatible may not meet this criterion, and hence, you never meet them. They, in turn, may just assume that you would never be interested in someone who didn't have a perfect body. The long and short of it is that it can create a scenario that makes it difficult to form a relationship based solely on authenticity and emotional connection.

Visual cues will always be an important component of gay men's sexuality. The important lesson here is that you don't allow yourself to become consumed with achieving ever more erotic visual cues. The path this creates is ultimately lonely and emotionally unfulfilling.

No feeling lasts forever

Skill: When life isn't going as we expect and painful emotions are running high, we often tell ourselves that this feeling will last forever. Nothing could be further from the truth, as all feelings come and go, wax and wane, over time. Challenge your own thinking that because life isn't pleasant, this unpleasantness is going to last forever. Nothing lasts forever.

Background: In my training as a psychologist who often works with suicidal patients, I learned early on that suicide is "a permanent solution to a temporary problem." And while suicide might seem like an indication of an extreme problem, most psychological problems have some component of this same belief that "distress will last forever." You've never felt the same way about anything or anyone consistently over your life. Your feelings come and go, ebb and flow, changing with the unpredictable and unexpected turns of life. The simple but wise truth is that feelings change—they *always* change.

Dan first came to see me after he was released from the local hospital after a suicide attempt. Dan and his partner had adopted two beautiful children five years earlier, and through a series of events that involved copious amounts of cocaine for both men, the relationship spiraled out of control until the point that Dan was thrown out of the house and slapped with a restraining order so that he could no longer see the children. Dan was understandably despondent and desperate, and feeling no hope of relief, he made a rash, alcohol-enabled decision to take his own life.

During our first session, I asked Dan if he would feel differently about his life if he knew for a fact that within two years, he would be allowed access to his children. "Well, of course I would!" he responded with a look as if I had just asked the world's silliest question. "Then act as if this is true," I told him. He looked bewildered at my response.

When Dan returned for his next session, he got it. He realized that he had assumed that the chaos in his life would never resolve and he would always feel this heart-rending distress. But as life always does, it changes; and when it does, so do our feelings. Nothing, but nothing, lasts forever.

RELATIONSHIPS

Don't let your sexual tastes be the filter by which you allow people into your life

Skill: Actively fight the urge to reach out only to people you find physically attractive. A man's physical appearance has virtually nothing to do with who he is on the inside, his values, and what kind of friend he is likely to be.

Background: When Roger walks into a room, he scans it for men whom he finds attractive. It's not that he's looking to hook up with anyone necessarily, it's just his way. He has a thing for tall, strapping, dark-haired men. When he sees one, he finds a way to strike up a conversation, usually with the intent to hook up.

What Roger doesn't realize is that he looks past a dozen other people, both men and women, who don't fit into his sexual appetite. And while he means no ill, he looks right through them. His eyes communicate a slight boredom, and his conversation is often brief and thoughtless.

Roger's behavior is like that of so many gay men. Over the years, we have trained ourselves to always be on the lookout for men who might be potential sexual partners—even when we aren't actively looking for sex. I've known gay men who've been in committed relationships for years who surround themselves only with other men whom they find attractive.

I remember one Thanksgiving many years ago, I had a large group of friends over to my house for dinner. The day after, I got a call from one of the invitees, Greg, thanking me for dinner. As we talked, he noted that he had attempted to talk to another gay man, Robert, who worked in a similar profession. He attempted several times to start up a conversation, but each time he felt he was at best tolerated and, at worst, ignored. As the evening progressed, it became clear that Robert was interested in someone else at the dinner, a gay man with whom he eventually left.

What Robert never knew was that Greg wasn't interested in him sexually. He was, as it turns out, wanting to tell Robert about a position that had just been vacated in his company. It could have been a nice step forward in Robert's career, but Greg was so put off with Robert's behavior, the conversation never happened.

Later that same day, I spoke with Robert, who seemed oblivious to the fact that he had virtually ignored everyone at the party. When I asked him if he had met Greg, he couldn't remember.

Robert's behavior is not unique. When you start to notice it in yourself, you'll be surprised, maybe even shocked, to discover how often you fail to notice other people around you, especially when you're in the presence of someone you find attractive.

When you use your sexual appetite as a social filter, you miss a great many of the wonderful people who will cross your path. In fact, many of the better friends in your life will be those people with whom there isn't even a trace of sexual attraction.

The lesson here is to remember that when meeting people, you aren't casting a tableau of handsome men for your bedroom. Rather, you are looking for people with whom you find a satisfying emotional connection. These are the people who will fill your life with joy and abundant possibilities.

"Leading" with your sexual prowess is just one of the ways a gay man will start an inauthentic relationship. Within the body lies a man of complex and interesting emotional structure, but this is hidden behind the sexual charge of the moment. Men— and especially gay men—aren't noted for the ability to think rationally once the sexual energy is sparking. In those moments, you are likely to say whatever is necessary to make that person like you in return.

Be right, or be happy

Skill: Asserting your own ideas is important, but when you do so at the expense of relationships, you hurt yourself and diminish your experience. Before insisting that your way is the right way, ask yourself, How important is it that I be right—and at what cost? Sometimes backing down for the sake of another person's ego is more effective at creating happy relationships than being right or in control.

Background: Think about it carefully. Why has Judy Garland always had such a loyal and die-hard group of fans, even fifty years after her death? What fueled the behind-the-scenes rage toward Martha Stewart? Why do we still love and remember Elizabeth Taylor? All of these examples have one thing in common: people are sympathetic when they sense humanity in others and are put off when they see nothing but perfection. When you show only perfection, you create anxiety in others and play upon their own insecurities. The darker side of a person often wants to destroy the perfection that makes him or her look bad by comparison.

My client Jeff remodeled a wonderful old home in Key West. He put years into planning every detail of the house, down to the last fork and saucer in the kitchen. Everything was thought out and purchased specifically for the "look" of the house.

Sometime after the house was finished, he noticed that his friends were increasingly turning down his invitations to stay with him. He found out that they would travel to Key West and stay in a frumpy guesthouse or with another friend whose home wasn't nearly as lavish. He wondered what was really going on.

What Jeff didn't realize was that while people admired his attention to detail, the absolute insistence on perfection made them uncomfortable. It was like trying to spend a relaxing vacation while sleeping in a design museum, and the two were just incompatible. Jeff's perfection made others so nervous that they couldn't maintain things as he wished, so they opted to spend their Florida vacations in more comfortable and relaxed atmospheres.

The façade of perfection is sometimes a defense that the gay man develops during the early years of shame. To ward off and compensate for shame, he puts forth a flawless image. Unfortunately, that practice also distances himself from others. At the end of the day, what other people really connect with is another person's humanity, not his (or her) façade of perfection.

Let others see your mistakes. Be generous in admitting your shortcomings, failings, and social missteps. Be the first to take responsibility for your share of a conflict. If you will practice this consistently, you will find your life filled with loving and supportive people who make your life truly worthwhile.

Always look first for the innocence in others

Skill: See past the betrayal, anger, and dishonesty in others to find their core innocence. Other people hurt you because they are hurting. It is extraordinarily rare that anyone acts out of a desire to deliberately hurt another person. Most often when we hurt others, it's because we are acting out of our pain and are being mindless of the well-being of others.

Background: I can't remember when I first heard the phrase "contempt before investigation," but it stuck with me as it describes how I sometimes operate in the world. I immediately assume that another person has ill intent toward me when he or she may have no such thing in mind. How many times have I imagined that a friend, lover, business associate, or simply another driver on the road *intentionally* did something to upset me when, in fact, there were other reasons—sometimes really good reasons—for what they did, which had nothing to do with trying to upset me? When I default to ideas of contempt before investigating the true reasons for another person's behavior, I'm almost always wrong. And even if I'm not wrong, such an approach toward others puts me in a foul mood, and only hurts me and diminishes my joy.

Ultimately, I've come to believe that in each moment, we're all doing the best that we can. When I see life through this lens, I can allow others the space to be themselves, even when I've judged their behavior as inadequate or downright hurtful. When I challenge the belief that others are driven by ill intentions, and instead hold the dialectic that "he is doing the best that he can do," it lessens my anger and makes the mistakes of others more tolerable. When I walk through the world expecting others to be perfect, I am setting myself up for a miserable existence—for no one, including myself, comes close to perfect. Give the same level of forgiveness to others that you'd like to receive in return. If you do, you'll lessen your own distress immeasurably and increase your experience of joy.

In conflict, assess your responsibility first

Skill: Whenever you encounter a problem in a relationship, consider and verbalize your responsibility first before focusing on the perceived error of the other.

Background: It's an old habit from the days of shame, and it goes something like this: never admit a mistake unless you absolutely have to. When shame was charging at the door, even cracking it the slightest felt dangerous, as if the whole thing would come barreling down upon you. To admit that you were wrong brought up feelings of shame that could not be tolerated.

Now, in stage three, it's important to recognize this old habit that is based in shame. Whenever there is a problem, the first reaction is to blame someone else rather than take responsibility for your part of the problem. This is a tough habit to break and takes a great deal of practice to do so successfully.

Authentic living means that you take responsibility for your own actions. When those actions create problems, you can't escape by denying your responsibility. Owning up to your part *before* criticizing someone else will improve your relationships and strengthen your own self-esteem.

One of the issues that very often arises among gay male couples is the inability of either man to take responsibility for what is happening in the relationship. Each has his own story, and they sometimes become fortified in their positions, refusing to budge. This can create a disastrous impasse for the relationship.

Ray and Gordon came in for couples therapy. Each was clearly angry at the other, and both were wondering aloud if their relationship should be ended. After a few sessions, it became clear that the root of conflict was that Ray felt that Gordon didn't do much around the house, never prepared dinner, and was always working; and that Gordon felt that Ray didn't appreciate all the benefits they both enjoyed because of Gordon's high-paying job. Neither Ray nor Gordon was willing to admit any personal responsibility for their problems, and both were tenaciously determined to blame the other. At times, it seemed as if the therapy sessions were more about each man trying to win the therapist over to his side of the story rather than owning any part of the problem.

A quite unexpected shift occurred after several months of stalemate. At that session, Gordon started off by saying that he had thought a great deal about it and realized that he needed to improve his involvement in the relationship and reduce some of his traveling for business. It was as if a dam broke. Within no time, Ray was owning up to his persistent nagging of Gordon. From that point forward, the therapy made excellent strides and the two men were able to significantly improve their relationship.

On the surface it may seem overly simplistic, but it isn't. If you, as Gordon did, will own your responsibility in a conflict, it creates a safe place for the other person to own their responsibility. You don't own anything that isn't yours, but simply take responsibility for what may have been your contribution to the problem.

The lesson of taking responsibility first before placing blame would have eliminated a great deal of distress for Gordon and Ray. Sure, they would have still had their differences and occasional arguments, but the tone of their relationship would have been far more loving and supportive.

This lesson works wonders not just in intimate relationships but in all kinds of relationships. Take responsibility for your actions and other people may be angry at first, but in the long run they will respect and trust you. Whenever you are tempted to blame someone else, learn to pause and first ask yourself, "What

have I done to create this problem?" This will allow you to elim-
inate a great many conflicts in your life.

The essence of living with shame is in not owning your shortcomings and weaknesses. The only way to continue the distress
of shame is to minimize the experience of shame. Refusing to
admit to personal shortcomings is one way in which gay men
often learn to minimize the distress of shame. By owning your
own behavior, you not only live authentically but reduce the distress of shame. After all, once you own the injury, you realize
that there really isn't any shame in it at all.

Keep your inner circle sacred and safe

Skill: Allow only those people who are trustworthy into your
inner circle of intimacy. Too quickly trusting someone who
hasn't yet proved his or her trustworthiness is highly risky. This
skill is about being slow and selective in bringing other people
into a close level of intimacy.

Background: We all are susceptible to a contagion effect when
it comes to other people. No matter how strong-minded we may
be, we are vulnerable to the ideas and judgments of those people
with whom we maintain close relationships. Because of this contagion effect, it is in your best interest to surround yourself with
people who share your values and who inspire you to grow in life
and reach further than you might otherwise.

It's easy to find yourself surrounded by gay men you enjoy but
who are also judgmental and not necessarily supportive of authenticity. There's nothing inherently wrong with this, but a
steady diet of judgment, even when couched in humor, inevitably
feeds the judgmental tendency in all of us. Keep those friends at

arm's length and refuse to allow them a seat in the inner circle of your heart. After all, anyone who is judgmental of others will eventually be judgmental of you, despite the narcissistic belief that "I'm different and he'd never do that to me." A person who is judgmental, inauthentic, and unforgiving rarely discriminates.

Instead, deliberately seek out those friends who aspire to be better men and who are openly willing to own their own failures as well as successes. These are the men who will feed and inspire the highest part of you, and together, you will grow into the men you desire to be.

When John found himself single after a seven-year relationship with a successful public relations executive, he realized that if he wanted to change his life focus away from the materialism that colored his previous relationship, he would also have to change his circle of friends. After a year of attending local meditation groups, exercise classes, and volunteering at a hotline for gay youth, John had cultivated a new set of friends who were also interested in living authentically. As he looked back at those previous years, he noted, "I never realized how strong of an influence my ex and all our friends had over me. Having friends who walk a similar path makes all the difference."

In life, you will meet all types of people—many of whom are the antithesis of who you want to become. The problem isn't that these people exist, or even that you have met them. The issue is that you don't have to give them your number. Knowing who to let in and who to gently keep at a distance is an immensely important and necessary skill for positive growth. Surround yourself with only those people who share your values and whose behavior is consistent with the type of man you want to be, and gently let go of those friendships that aren't.

Validate what is valid (and never the invalid)

Skill: In a relationship, seek to validate what you perceive is valid in another person. Let him or her know what you respect in his behavior. Never give compliments that aren't true or are insincere, for we all have a sophisticated radar for detecting when someone is patronizing us and when they are sincere.

Background: An important skill in maintaining any relationship is learning to validate the other person. In fact, validation is what makes a good relationship mutually satisfying.

The lesson in validation is that you always validate the valid and never the invalid. What this means is you acknowledge or praise only those things that are good and appropriate but never those things that are not. An easy pitfall to fall into is to be overly validating in a relationship, which is likely to be perceived as patronizing by the other person.

Maintaining authenticity in relationships requires that you are always on the lookout for what is valid in the other person. For example, if your lover comes home and rants about how badly he was treated at work, but you sense that he may be deserving of some of this distress, you can validate him by not agreeing that he was wronged but by agreeing that it is stressful to be in such a situation. In this case, you would have validated what you believed was valid.

Why validating the valid is important to authenticity is because gay men who enter stage three sometimes take the path of trying to be overly accepting and supportive of the people around them. At the time, this may feel like a good strategy for building solid, emotionally connected relationships. Unfortunately, it is a strategy that most often backfires. Other people are suspicious of someone who is too validating, and they eventually begin discounting anything that person validates.

While authenticity involves such things as adopting a non-judgmental stance and no longer seeing others as mere sexual objects, it does not mean total and complete acceptance of everyone you meet. The most authentic person learns to find what is true and honest in another person, call that out, and support it.

Own your side of the street

Skill: You are responsible for your feelings and only your feelings (not anyone else's). Take responsibility for your feelings without pushing them off onto others (i.e., "I feel unattractive." vs. "You make me feel unattractive.")

Background: While it may not be apparent on the surface, this skill strikes at one of the core ways in which shame has shaped us as gay men. Because so many of us learned to live our lives according to the expectations of others (rather than following our own dreams), we became experts at holding other people responsible for our feelings. As the years progressed and you came out of the closet, this troubling habit of abandoning yourself, accepting other people's feelings as more valid, and consequently holding other people responsible for how you feel continued. The truth is that your feelings, values, and dreams are just as valid as anyone else's. Learning to assert and own your feelings, even when you perceive that others may not accept or approve of them, is a critical turning point in overcoming the ill effects of toxic shame.

The skill of "owning your side of the street" is all about knowing what you feel, expressing those feelings honestly, and taking responsibility for your feelings without blaming others. Other people can have a strong influence on you, but ultimately you are in control of how you feel. This is one of the great insights that psychotherapy has to offer—simply, you are not a victim to your feelings. You are in control of how you feel.

Steve complained often about how his partner made him feel "shut down" and "small." Steve had a good job running a small bed and breakfast in San Francisco, and his boyfriend Peter was a highly successful film producer. The couple had a whirlwind romance after first meeting, and everything seemed to work perfectly between them until they had been together for about a year. That's when Steve started to feel that he was somehow "less than" Peter. Over a year of therapy, it became apparent Steve had a history of feeling inferior to the men he dated that stemmed all the way back to always feeling as if he never measured up to his overachieving brother in his parents' eyes. As Steve began to embrace the reality that his feelings of inferiority were *his feelings* and not the responsibility of Peter, he quite naturally began to feel better about his relationship with Peter.

Speak to the offender first (instead of everyone else)

Skill: When experiencing conflict in a relationship, express your feelings to the person with whom you have the conflict rather than talking about the conflict with other people.

Background: Werner Erhardt, the enigmatic and controversial founder of EST (a self-help seminar that swept the world in the 1970s), was famous for asking this question: "When you have a conflict with someone, who is the first person with whom you discuss this?" Of course, reason tells you that you would likely discuss it with the person with whom you have the conflict. Experience, for most of us, says something quite different.

Many gay men have a habit of talking about conflicts with everyone around them *except* the person with whom they have the conflict. Why is this?

I believe one of the roots of this troubling habit can be found in the deeply held belief that we can't trust our own experience to be valid. Therefore, when we find ourselves in conflict, we go about seeking the validation of other people to help bolster our own position. By the time we actually get around to confronting the person with whom we have the conflict, we have involved several other people, asking them to support our side, and inevitably making the conflict worse.

The habit of involving other people in our relationship conflicts can be truly devastating, especially when the conflict involves a romantic relationship. We mobilize our friends and polarize their feelings about the relationship, so that they believe we have been unduly mistreated and our partner is the one to blame. This puts into motion a troubling scenario where friends of one person in a couple develop strong negative opinions about the other person. The tension and conflict that then develop around the couple have ended more than a few gay male relationships.

One of the most difficult things to do when you are struggling with your own internal shame is to deal with someone with whom you have a conflict. Your natural urge is to gather reinforcements about you to help you through the battle. The more effective practice, when shame is no longer the driving issue, is to unlearn this behavior by mindfully keeping a conflict solely between you and the other person. Regardless of whether you resolve the conflict or not, you have not dragged your friends into the fray needlessly and escalated the conflict. In the end, the conflict stands a much better chance of successful resolution without the involvement of well-meaning bystanders.

Authenticity is difficult when you are galvanizing support from others for your side of the story. The very nature of the task demands that you paint the person with whom you have the conflict in a particularly negative way, and yourself as being somewhat blameless. The motive is often to draw love and support toward you by demeaning the other person.

Authenticity, in contrast, requires that you acknowledge yourself as clearly and wholly as possible, including both strengths and weaknesses. Because most conflicts between people are created by both persons, authenticity requires a certain level of honesty about your own participation in the conflict that isn't entirely consistent with the objective of winning others' support. In short, you slant the story to your benefit in order to be convincing.

Live in integrity

Skill: Always strive to be as honest as possible, even when it may seem to be easier or more efficient to hide the truth. Avoid giving others an inaccurate impression even when you haven't done anything deliberately to create that impression.

Background: I sat in astonishment. Was I actually hearing what she said? I was attending a meeting of gay and lesbian psychotherapists in the San Francisco Bay area when one of the therapists said, "I'm not always certain that telling the truth is a good idea."

On the agenda of the seminar meeting were several topics, and this one in particular had to do with couples telling one another about infidelities they had while together. This therapist was voicing what I had once believed: "Better to protect the relationship if honesty will break it apart." But for me, it had been years since I believed that honesty could sometimes be a bad idea. I've now changed my mind.

Any therapist who works with men in relationships, and gay men in particular, had better be ready to handle the surprise phone call that sometimes goes something like this: "Hello? Hmmm. I forgot to mention something in our last couples session. Well, huh, I don't know quite how to say this. It will really hurt him (her). I didn't mean it to hurt. I mean, oh well, let me just say it: I've been having an affair."

After years of patching together couples in therapy and coaching one partner that "some secrets are best kept," I began to notice something astonishing. The couples who seemed to keep secrets often grew further apart and rarely stayed together in the end. Was I doing them any favors by encouraging one of them to "protect" the other from the truth?

What I've come to see in my practice is that secrets create emotional distance. It's sort of like two parallel lines that are running very close to each other. Suddenly, one changes trajectory by just a fraction of a degree. At first, you hardly notice the distance. In time, the distance grows and the two lines move farther and farther apart. One small, tightly held secret can sometimes be all that it takes to drive two otherwise loving people apart.

If you're like I once was, maybe you're thinking, "But isn't it true that what you don't know can't hurt you?" If that were true in life, HIV wouldn't be a worldwide problem and ignorance of all sorts would be bliss. It just isn't so.

You are forced to view the world through the lens of your own being. You can't escape the truths you know, even if you do keep them from your partner or friends. The very fact that you know something to be true creates an effect on you and your behavior.

In the instance of marital infidelity, you know that you cheated even if your partner doesn't. That knowledge is enough of a wedge to push the two of you apart, even ever so slightly. It erodes your trust in yourself and in the relationship, and it can even begin to destroy your trust in your partner (i.e., "If I'm keeping this secret, imagine what he's keeping from me!").

Authenticity demands truthfulness. Opinions, passing feelings, judgments, and hunches, when not supported by any facts, are often best kept to one's self. After all, feelings change and hunches are often wrong. But when you know the facts, those never change. Where facts are concerned, absolute and radical honesty is always best.

When I think about the importance of honesty, my mind often wanders back to those old episodes of the *Bob Newhart Show* where he worked as a psychologist and often held group therapy sessions. One character would tell another character that he "hated" her because she gave him a mean look when he walked in. From there, the group would erupt into chaos, and Bob was always there to point out the humor in it all.

Those groups were not honest. They were impulsive expressions of feelings. To understand the difference, you must think of feelings passing over you like waves. At one point in the day, you may be enraged with your spouse for not picking up the dry cleaning, and at another point, proud of him for having earned a great promotion at work. Feelings ebb and flow, washing over you and then subsiding. Only when you have observed a feeling reoccurring consistently over time can you conclude that it is a fair representation about how you "feel" about something or someone.

Honesty is often confused with the dangerous practice of expressing impulsive feelings in the moment. The kind of honesty that is the bedrock of authenticity isn't about impulsive feelings,

rather, it is truthfulness about observable facts and those enduring feelings that are consistent over time. So telling off your
boyfriend because he was late to pick you up isn't what honesty
is all about. However, telling your boyfriend that you find his
consistent pattern of tardiness troublesome is.

Honesty is not an excuse to deliberately hurt others or to express pent-up rage. Saying things like "don't you know that no one
likes you" or "everyone thinks you're *way* too bossy" isn't being
honest. Statements like these are filled with passive-aggressive
intent and are meant to hurt the recipient. Honesty is meant to
help the recipient stay more connected with reality, and the only
way to achieve this is to "stick with facts."

The important lesson here is that protecting others from the
truth of the facts isn't "protecting" them at all. As I mentioned
earlier, when you "protect" another person from the truth, it's
more likely that you're protecting yourself and your pride.

The practice of honesty is difficult to start, especially when
you grow up learning to hide the more shameful parts of yourself. It feels threatening to reveal that you have made a mistake,
taken something or someone for granted, or deliberately done
something that you knew was wrong. To say these things brings
up vivid memories of shame and a vague sense that you are a bad
person and will ultimately be rejected by everyone around you.

Once the gay man has tackled and diminished the toxic shame
in his life, he is better equipped for the practice of honesty. He is
no longer scared of what the truth might reveal about himself to
others. He is presenting his true self to everyone, and there's no
shame in it at all.

Authenticity builds relationships that are satisfying and emotionally fulfilling. Any relationship that is riddled with secrets
and omissions will not be emotionally fulfilling.

Default to forgiveness rather than resentment

Skill: Always seek to allow others the space to be imperfect. And when others disappoint you, avoid the temptation to keep an accounting of such disappointments.

Background: When I hold resentment toward another person, it is almost always rooted in my fantasy of who I believe that person should be—and my own resistance to accepting him or her as is. When I fully accept another person, I do my best to see him with a clear lens, one that isn't fogged by my own expectations, beliefs, and projections. When I resent another person, I am holding rigidly to my own expectations and fantasies of that person as if to say, "You shouldn't be the person who you are."

You may believe, for example, that your neighbor is terribly arrogant and unfriendly because he rarely speaks or acknowledges you on the street. If, however, you find out that your neighbor's partner recently died and then a month later he lost his job, you might think differently, right? Accepting others is all about allowing someone else the space to be who they are without you layering judgments and interpretations on top of their behavior. Your neighbor may act unfriendly, but he also has some very understandable reasons for being withdrawn and quiet.

Jamey came into therapy with his partner, Andrew, because he was concerned that he wasn't more sexually interested in his partner, whom he loved dearly and to whom, at least intellectually, he was attracted. Jamey just never felt the urge to be intimate with his partner and even had some feelings of repulsion toward sex. Jamey's partner was tired of asking for sex and being turned down, so their sex life had dwindled to nothing more than cuddling for almost a year. Andrew had been very kind and understanding about this situation but in recent months had become very concerned that Jamey wasn't attracted to him—not to mention frustrated that he hadn't had his own needs met in quite some time. Andrew, convinced that something deeper was wrong with the relationship—even that Jamey was having an affair—had privately decided to move out of the house if things didn't improve. Jamey hadn't been willing to talk about his low desire for sex with Andrew, and likewise, Andrew, fearing rejection, hadn't been willing to bring it up, either.

As part of my assessment of this couple, I requested that Jamey have his testosterone levels measured, and as I suspected, his testosterone was so low as to almost be immeasurable. Within days of Jamey starting testosterone supplementation therapy, his sex drive came roaring back. Needless to say, Andrew was surprised, pleased, and a bit confused, as he had convinced himself that Jamey was no longer attracted to him.

What Jamey and Andrew experienced holds great wisdom for the rest of us. There are good reasons for our behavior even when we don't know what those reasons are. In Jamey's case, he suffered from a deficit in the male hormone that fuels sexual interest, and not, as Andrew had imagined, a waning love for his partner. Thankfully, the couple hadn't broken up and came in for help, just in the nick of time. The story we tell ourselves about other people's behavior, much like the story Andrew had created, may have little connection to reality; and yet we can become utterly convinced of its accuracy. Forgiveness, as a skill, is deeply rooted in our ability to let go of our most treasured fantasies and accept reality as it is, and not as we wish it to be. When we truly and radically accept reality, we loosen the commitment to the story in our heads and, instead, embrace the facts without judgment. As in the case of Jamey and Andrew, our stories about other people are often full of errors, omissions, and exaggerations.

Defaulting to forgiveness means that we accept that other people have good reasons for their behavior, even when we may not know those reasons or agree with them. Each of us is just trying to get through life as best we can, and forgiveness is the essence of allowing others the space to follow their own inner voice even when we disagree with it.

Forgiveness means that "I allow you to not live up to my fantasies"; it does not mean you continue to allow someone to hurt you, take advantage of you, or repeatedly invalidate you. Defaulting to forgiveness is also not the same thing as allowing that person back into your inner circle of intimacy. Forgiveness is all about my willingness to accept the truth about you without expectations or judgment. As Marianne Williamson often says in her lectures, "Just because you forgive someone doesn't mean you're going to lunch together anytime soon."

Embrace ambivalence

Skill: We rarely, if ever, feel just one way about virtually anything in life. You and I are ambivalent creatures—we naturally have competing feelings. Allow yourself permission to hold competing feelings without denying or forcing feelings that are inconvenient or unpleasant for the sake of premature clarity.

Background: Our modern culture, with its emphasis on immediate gratification, often demands that you feel only one feeling about most anything in life and discourages any mention of ambivalence. Even simple things, like a customer satisfaction survey, require that you rate your satisfaction with one number, versus expressing ambivalence such as "I enjoyed the meal very much except for the salad, which was bland and uninteresting." When it comes to the big things in life, like relationships, ambivalence is not only discouraged, it's often seen as a sign of relationship failure; so we subtly learn to not express contrary feelings and to keep them private.

Who hasn't felt both love and anger toward the same person? Boredom and excitement? Frustration and pleasure? The reality of our emotional landscape is that it is full of competing feelings. When we fail to fully embrace and allow for ambivalence, those feelings we hide don't disappear, and sometimes they even grow until we can no longer hide them. When this happens, we can hurt other people by seeming to suddenly change how we feel about them, when in fact, the change wasn't sudden at all but rather something that we hid from view until we were no longer able to suppress it.

When you begin to feel uncomfortable with a relationship, perhaps as if the other person no longer really knows you, it's often because of your failure to fully express your own ambivalence. Over time, ambivalence that isn't embraced causes two people to pull apart. The more we hide and "clean up" our feelings for the benefit of another person, the greater the distance between us grows.

Johnny didn't want to hurt his boyfriend's feelings by telling him that he really didn't enjoy spending every minute of every weekend together. It's true, Johnny enjoyed his boyfriend's company and was just as often the one who would suggest activities for the two of them to enjoy, like hiking together, going to the beach, or working out. But sometimes, he just wanted to stay in his own apartment and do things separately with his friends. In therapy, Johnny expressed his fear that if he told his boyfriend he wanted to spend time in his own apartment or with friends, his boyfriend would see this as a sign that the relationship wasn't going well. I encouraged Johnny to find a validating way to express his need for time alone to his boyfriend, such as simply telling him that he wanted some private time and that this need had nothing to do with how he felt about the relationship. The next week, Johnny came back to therapy amazed to report that his boyfriend not only wasn't offended but stated that he wanted the same. The two had spent a wonderful Saturday together and then had Sunday apart. Johnny stated that not only did he have a great weekend, he was really looking forward to having dinner together with his boyfriend later that week.

Perhaps this may be somewhat simplistic, but as in most things in life, it is the simple things that often create the most trouble. Where is it written that couples must spend every available moment together? Or that a gay man in a committed relationship can't find another man really attractive? Or that saying "no" to your partner's request for sex is a bad thing? It's true in life generally, but particularly in relationships, that we must be free to express our ambivalence even with the small things if we are to maintain positive feelings. The denial of uncomfortable, disagreeable, or less than positive feelings is often the root from which a deeper, more malicious discontent grows. Without darkness, light has no meaning—likewise, love has little meaning when you have not experienced competing feelings.

We don't really believe the flowery sentiments displayed in Hallmark cards. Rarely do phrases on bumper stickers change our lives. Affirmations of self-worth often don't change how we feel about ourselves, no matter how many times we quote them. Why? Mostly because we don't believe simplistic statements of feelings as we instinctively know that the most important things in life trigger ambivalence within us. Embrace your ambivalence, especially in relationships, and you'll find that you reach a new, powerful level of authenticity that ultimately makes your relationships stronger and more fulfilling.

CHARTING YOUR PRACTICE

Using these skills is a daily practice. Each new day presents new opportunities for authenticity and skillful growth. Following is a chart that lists each of the skills and provides space for you to note if you practice the skill. This chart can be particularly helpful as a tool to summarize and remind you of the skills at the end of each day and to document your progress.

Many *Velvet Rage* groups have found the chart to be a very helpful tool for each group member to complete and bring to the weekly meeting. *Velvet Rage* groups are often structured with a time for reading a section of the book and discussing the material. Afterward, time is allotted for each group member to share how he used the skills in daily activities. The chart provides an efficient tool to summarize the group member's week and to help him remember what skills he used and how those skills helped him to live more authentically.

Skill	Description	Practice (circle if "yes")							Notes
Life Choices									
The man I would become.	Make decisions based upon what the man you wish to become would do in the same situation.	Sun	Mon	Tues	Wed	Thur	Fri	Sat	
Inner peace above all else.	Ultimately, the only goal of life is inner peace. How does this choice contribute to your inner peace?	Sun	Mon	Tues	Wed	Thur	Fri	Sat	
Never react while feeling an intense emotion.	Delay making a decision or reacting while feeling an intense emotion. Distract yourself until the feeling subsides, then decide what decision or actions should be taken.	Sun	Mon	Tues	Wed	Thur	Fri	Sat	
Contentment over approval.	Populate your life with investments of time and emotion that increase your contentment rather than eliciting acceptance and approval from others.	Sun	Mon	Tues	Wed	Thur	Fri	Sat	
Increasing Positive Emotions									
Accept reality on reality's terms.	Seek to see reality as it is rather than as you wish it to be.	Sun	Mon	Tues	Wed	Thur	Fri	Sat	
One thing, one person, one conversation in the moment.	Give your full attention and focus to that which is before you in this moment.	Sun	Mon	Tues	Wed	Thur	Fri	Sat	
Take a nonjudgmental stance whenever possible.	Limit the urge to classify everything in life somewhere between good and bad. "It is what it is."	Sun	Mon	Tues	Wed	Thur	Fri	Sat	
Obsessing about pain creates more pain.	The continuous recitation of painful feelings, stories, and memories brings only temporary relief and, in the long term, increases your pain.	Sun	Mon	Tues	Wed	Thur	Fri	Sat	
Walk your way out of distress.	When feeling particularly distressing emotions, the only way to decrease the pain is to force yourself to act contrary to the emotion.	Sun	Mon	Tues	Wed	Thur	Fri	Sat	
Respect your body.	Care for your body as a precious possession.	Sun	Mon	Tues	Wed	Thur	Fri	Sat	
No feeling lasts forever.	Emotions are only temporary, and all will eventually pass.	Sun	Mon	Tues	Wed	Thur	Fri	Sat	

Skill	Description	Practice (circle if "yes")	Notes
Relationships			
Don't let your sexual tastes be the filter by which you allow people into your life.	Approach and cultivate relationships with people who are authentic and validating rather than just those who are sexually interesting.	Sun Mon Tues Wed Thur Fri Sat	
Be right, or be happy.	Relinquish the urge to always be "right," and instead attend to the needs of your relationships.	Sun Mon Tues Wed Thur Fri Sat	
Always look first for the innocence in others.	No matter how difficult another person may be, he is doing in that moment the best he can do.	Sun Mon Tues Wed Thur Fri Sat	
In conflict, always assess your responsibility first.	Resist the urge to blame another for a conflict, and instead first assess and own your responsibility.	Sun Mon Tues Wed Thur Fri Sat	
Keep your inner circle sacred and safe.	Carefully guard and assess those individuals you allow into your inner circle of intimacy. Their influence is monumental.	Sun Mon Tues Wed Thur Fri Sat	
Validate what is valid (and never the invalid)	Seek to find the truth in another person's experience and reflect that back to him or her.	Sun Mon Tues Wed Thur Fri Sat	
Own your side of the street.	Own your feelings. No one else is responsible for how you feel.	Sun Mon Tues Wed Thur Fri Sat	
Speak to the offender first (instead of everyone else).	In a conflict, seek to speak to the offender before discussing the conflict with others.	Sun Mon Tues Wed Thur Fri Sat	
Live in integrity.	In all interactions with others, be radically and deliberately honest.	Sun Mon Tues Wed Thur Fri Sat	
Default to forgiveness rather than resentment.	When disappointed or offended by others, allow the other person to hold a different point of view rather than closing your heart to him or her.	Sun Mon Tues Wed Thur Fri Sat	
Embrace ambivalence.	Seek out and embrace the omnipresent competing feelings about all things in life.	Sun Mon Tues Wed Thur Fri Sat	

Epilogue

THIS PETER PAN
GROWS UP

"You can't catch me and make me a man."

PETER PAN

I stepped out into the fog that night not quite sure of what was next. The thick soup of San Francisco dampness that descends upon the city on most summer nights was particularly heavy, and I tripped over something on the sidewalk, but this night it didn't really matter what it was. My mind was racing, yet my thoughts had not budged since I heard the words: "HIV-positive." At least, that's what the teary-eyed nurse just told me. Like a good southern boy, I awkwardly thanked her, turned on my heels, and walked down the sickeningly fluorescent-lit hallway praying I would reach darkness before my river of tears burst its dam. I reached the bus stop—God knows how long I had wandered the streets—but only in time to see the taillights of the last bus of the night slipping into the misty darkness. I awoke slumped on the steps of the doorway to my small apartment that overlooked the Castro with waves of fog wafting over me. I remember thinking, "So this is how it ends."

Life changed for me that night some twenty-five years ago; but at the time, I would have no idea just where it would take me. I assumed, as did most everyone else in the late 1980s, that HIV was inevitably a terminal diagnosis. As a young man of twenty-six years, bewitched by the narcissism of youth, I had foolishly believed that my life was infinite. Now I considered that I would die, probably sooner rather than later. This, in the days and weeks after that night in the San Francisco fog, I would come to accept as fact.

And why wouldn't I? As a young therapist with a newly crafted PhD, I had already seen much devastation from the HIV epidemic. Young men were going blind, using canes to tap their way down streets lined with gay bars. Others were slipping into eternal idiocy with dementia. Still others went to work one day, fell ill the next, and were laid to rest within the same week. "Where is John?" is a question even I knew never to ask. If someone suddenly disappeared from the scene, you just assumed he had succumbed to the plague.

That was more than two decades ago; fortunately for me, a combination of good genes, perhaps a weak strain of the virus, and the invention of the "cocktail" in 1996 turned my near-death experience into a manageable chronic illness. I was one of the very lucky ones who narrowly escaped with my life.

Only now have I come to understand the profound impact that virus has had on who I was and what I have become. It gave me my life to live in a hurry. I had places to go, people to meet, jobs to treasure and quit, and many miles to travel before the darkness descended. Though it would seem the diagnosis of a terminal disease would make one grow up quickly, I did quite the opposite and became an out-of-control adolescent-man. I left no stone unturned, no wine untasted.

For the better part of ten years, I lived under a cloud of a temporary future. Before the HIV "cocktail" of medications, no one knew how long it would take for the virus to ultimately destroy my immune system. After the cocktail, we all wondered when the clever virus would outsmart the antiviral medication and again invade our immune systems, as it had for the unlucky ones.

As it turned out, those dire futures never materialized for me, but I wouldn't come to trust this until the century rolled over. In that time, I lived in a state of fast-forward, always trying to get the very best—or at least the quickest high—out of life before the final fog descended. I demanded that life deliver everything I wanted. The clicking of my viral clock was loud and undeniable. I had nothing, neither time nor love, to waste.

It would seem that if you are facing the potential end of your life, you might turn your attention to more serious matters, such as the meaning and substance of your life. Who hasn't at one time or another played the parlor game of "What would you do if you had only a year to live?" to which most of us respond with something about spending more time with the people we love or being of service in some meaningful way. I responded by burying my head in the sand, refusing to seek medical attention for HIV, fleeing from any perceived responsibility, and doing everything I could to avoid pain and seek pleasure. The adolescent in me flourished, and the man I would become remained buried and undeveloped. As adolescent boys do, I was the center of my own world, and others were welcomed into that world only if they could make me feel good. And just as soon as the good feelings faded, so did my use for the relationship. Like Peter Pan, I reveled in my boyish ways and stubbornly refused to grow up.

With these hounds of time and mortality nipping at my heels, I dove into my own life and my work with two goals in mind: (1) make money, and (2) sleep with as many men as possible. I worked for companies like Hewlett Packard, Pacific Gas and Electric, and Dayton Hudson (now known as Target) as a "corporate" psychologist whose job it was to help manage the workforces of these corporate giants with an element of kindness and humanity. More accurately, I mostly ran a charm school for executives, which we called leadership training, and orchestrated large-scale layoffs of underperforming and/or overpaid employees. I traveled widely and made a very good living that afforded me a small taste of the high life. From workshops in Aspen, Colorado, and committee meetings on the beach in Big Sur to presentations before corporate boards in the private, wood-paneled clubs of New York City, I did it all. I hated my work—but I assumed that everyone else did, too. During these years of blowing and going, spending and spinning, there were moments of questioning myself and what my life had become; but for the most part, it would be almost a decade before I would really stand up and take notice.

My moment of clarity came in the most unexpected way. I had just landed at the Phoenix airport and had taken a taxi to the local site of the company for whom I was then working. My job, as it had evolved, was primarily designing and executing corporate layoffs. It was quite an operation, as we had to orchestrate the cutting of final paychecks, off-site counseling centers, and security escorts for the dismissed employees. All of it had to happen like clockwork, with as little impact as possible to the remaining workforce. If we did our jobs well, those fated employees seemed to just vanish into thin air—one moment you see him sitting in his cubicle and the next his desk is clean and not a trace of his existence remains behind to trouble the survivors. As I walked into the lobby of the office building where I and my staff would be laying off employees the next day, the receptionist, whom I had never met, looked up and quite calmly asked, "Are we clubbing baby seals today?"

Within two weeks of that day, I quit that job—and I ended my corporate career. I had been trained as a psychologist, not to be a compassionate executioner. Money, achievement, success— these things didn't matter so much anymore. I needed to find something meaningful and passionate, and I had no time to waste. I was already more than five years past the date of my original diagnosis, and the accepted belief at the time was that one might have maybe seven years after seroconversion before succumbing to full-blown AIDS. If I was going to change my life, I had to act quickly.

I began volunteering a few hours a week for a local AIDS organization that provided counseling to both patients with AIDS and their families. Once a week I would veer off the highway that had once taken me to my job in Silicon Valley and drive to the cheerless halls of San Francisco General's AIDS Ward. There I would sit by the bed of a patient, and we would talk about life, love, family, and death. Even in the darkest of those encounters, there was something in the eyes of those who lingered between breath and stillness that brought me peace. I could sense their deep gratitude that someone had taken time to listen—really listen to their stories. In each hollow cheek and trembling bed, I saw myself, knowing that it was only a matter of time before I would be there, too. There was something magical about touching the pain buried within the hearts of these young men that seemed to help them, and it left an indelible impression on me.

Whatever it was that happened on those evenings, I knew that I had to find a way to get more of it into my life. To say it brought me joy may seem too strong, but it was most definitely a humble and abiding contentment. It would be years later that I would come to understand that it was this deeply abiding feeling of fulfillment that was my best guide to finding a passionate life.

In the retelling of my story, I find myself slipping at times into my own heroic fantasy in which I somewhat prophetically discover the secret to a fulfilling life and radically change my life for the better. But if I'm honest, I must admit that's not what really happened. Truth is, I had pushed myself both physically and emotionally beyond any reasonable limits, and I was utterly exhausted that day in Phoenix—not to mention very angry and disillusioned with my boss, whom I had come to see as an immoral corporate sellout. The quitting of my job was as much a personal temper tantrum as an enlightened choice. I was tired, pissed off, and scared of my future but more scared to die without having really lived.

Not long after I quit, the money ran out, leading to some rather drastic changes in my life. No longer could I afford the comfortable San Francisco house on the hill, the dinners out, or any of the other lifestyle features that go along with a corporate salary. Within six months, my partner and I relocated to a comfortable but very affordable "shotgun" just off Magazine Street in New Orleans. Here we could stretch our meager savings and buy mostly time to recover and rebuild our lives.

My partner at the time was a struggling artist who had enjoyed a few moments of notoriety in the art world but not enough to make a living from his paintings. He, unlike me, had never really struggled with finding his passion in life. He loved more than anything to make paintings, and he had never abandoned that love except when forced to take part-time jobs to support himself at a local deli or in a gallery selling the works of artists he had once studied in art school. In New Orleans, where time and rent were affordable, he could paint full-time, and I began chasing my recurring dream of writing a book about my experiences as a psychologist in the corporate world.

Within eighteen months' time, we went from living a plentiful life in San Francisco to floundering in the sweltering heat of New Orleans. I wrote furiously, sending off manuscript after manuscript, hoping to publish something—anything that would help me build the all-important resume of a writer. Everything I had read for aspiring authors said virtually the same thing: if you want to be published as a writer, you have to already have been published. (If you're thinking that sounds crazy and circular, it is. But nonetheless, it is the most common advice given to beginning writers even today.) I turned every intriguing thought or memory I had into an article for publication and rushed it off to the mailbox. Surely somewhere, someone would want to publish me. And after almost two years and literally hundreds of rejection letters, it happened. The *Christian Science Monitor*, which at the time was going through a corporate downsizing of its own, asked to publish an article I wrote under the title "Memoirs of a Corporate Executioner." The business editor, who was clearly more distraught over his own company's pending layoffs than he was enamored with my insights, published the article as a backhanded rebuttal to his managing editor. Then, shortly after publication, the *Los Angeles Times* republished the article in syndication, and, much to my amazement, within days a New York book editor with a smoker's voice and cynical laugh called and asked if I would be interested in turning the article into a book. Would I!

I was finally on my way. With half of a $5,000 advance in my hand, I went to work writing my first book. I eventually took an office in the French Quarter that I shared with another writer who was at the time the food critic for the local newspaper, the *Times-Picayune*. I spent my early mornings riding my bike down the tree-lined avenues of the Garden District and the Creole-inspired Esplanade Boulevard, which ended at the entrance of the New Orleans Museum of Art. There, I found the Rene Magritte painting that would become the cover of my first book. Afternoons were sometimes spent sitting in the fabled eateries of New Orleans, sampling the fare and sipping Sazeracs while my office mate would chat up the chef, be it Emeril Lagasse or Susan Spicer, while the waitstaff treated us like royalty, knowing that their very jobs depended upon whatever kind remarks might be published in the following day's review. Little did they know I was just thrilled to be dining off a menu that I couldn't have otherwise afforded.

Before I published my first writings, nothing was more discouraging than reading the story of a writer that would begin with something along the lines of "as luck would have it . . ." Was luck the only secret to becoming a successful writer? Surely there had to be something more. And if not, how does one go about acquiring this luck? I found those well-meaning stories so utterly demoralizing. But now, I must say, it *was* as luck would have it. Coinciding with the publication of my first book, *Corporate Executions: The Ugly Truth About Layoffs—How Corporate Greed Is Shattering Lives, Companies, and Communities*, AT&T conducted the largest single layoff—40,000 employees—that was ever recorded. My book was thus propelled to the top of the news, and I was subsequently doing interviews for CBS's *Sunday Morning*, the *NBC Nightly News*, and *60 Minutes*. Publications including the *New York Times*, *Wall Street Journal*, and *San Francisco Chronicle* ran articles about my book and my personal story of having been a corporate "executioner."

As it turned out, my value as a "media voice" was greater than as a writer. Despite being a frequent commentator on just about every talk and business show of the day, the sales of my book were mediocre. Nonetheless, I finally had my "writer's resume" and had established myself as a presentable, media-capable author.

It's hard to pinpoint the day, month, or even year when it happened, but somewhere in all of the bright lights of television studios and the limo rides between airports and radio stations, I once again forgot about those moments of bedside contentment in San Francisco. The siren's call of momentary fame and the promise of writing the next best seller hijacked my plans for the future. I was once again seduced by the fantasy of success rather than the quiet comfort of contentment.

I published several more books, each one a successive attempt to charm the publicity gods and achieve best-seller status, over the next few years. I moved from New Orleans to New York City, then to Key West, Florida, and ultimately to Santa Fe, New Mexico. A best seller remained just beyond my reach, and my limited fame proved to be as fickle as the stock market itself, ebbing and flowing with the angst of the times.

In 1996, the plague that had personally taken a home in my veins took a turn for the worse. My life partner fell seriously ill with pneumocystis pneumonia. He had gone in to the doctor that morning with what we thought was bad chest congestion and was admitted into the hospital that afternoon with a potentially terminal illness. I was scheduled to begin the book tour for my second book, *Beyond the Looking Glass*, the next day. Racked with anxiety over his health, my own dark future—for I was quite certain I would soon follow him into the hospital and likely the grave—and feeling the pressure of my publishing company, which had spent a great deal of money to arrange the book tour,

I arranged for a friend from San Francisco to stay with my partner in Key West while I began the tour. Miraculously (and there is no hyperbole here), protease inhibitors had just been approved by the FDA for the treatment of HIV. Like Lazarus rising from the tomb, within days of receiving this new medication my partner came back from the edge of death and soon returned to work in the old beer locker he had converted into a painting studio.

Unfortunately, although the new medications could bar the plague from the door, they did nothing to quell the rising existential anxiety that was coming to a boil in those of us who had buried more friends and lovers before the age of thirty than most people will in a lifetime. Life, it seemed, had played a cruel hoax on so many of us. Out of our tightly clenched fists it wrestled our lust for life and dangled us above a painful and horrible death. Then, on a whim, it simply ducked, turned on its heels, and mockingly laughed. How were we to ever trust life again?

In 1997 I encountered another unexpected turn in the road. On July 2, I received a call from my cousin's partner, Sylvia, that she was dead. Dead? At age forty-two? "But she's a lesbian," I remember thinking as Sylvia and I ended the call. "They don't get AIDS." For Betty Lynne, it wasn't AIDS but her diabetes that took her. I was more devastated by her death than anything I can remember before or since. She was the only person in my large family that truly accepted me as a gay man. She was my rock, my soul, my conscience. Until her death we had spoken by phone virtually daily. I could feel the dark, ugly mire of bitterness and resentment rising in me. Would everything—virtually anything—that meant something to me be ripped from my tattered life?

The last time I saw Betty Lynne was just a week before Sylvia unexpectedly found her dead on the kitchen floor clutching

Thich Nhat Hanh's book *On Becoming Peace.* It had been a particularly clear and warm evening in June, and we sat on the deck
outside the house looking up at the stars. As we sat for hours,
talking as we often did, she said at one point, "Whichever one of
us goes first will be the guardian angel of the other." I had no way
of knowing at the time how important those words would be to
me—and still are today.

The day Betty Lynne died, I called my parents, who were
preparing to leave on vacation, to tell them that their niece had
died. My mother, not one to allow much to interrupt her plans—
much less the sure-to-be-uncomfortable funeral of her lesbian
niece—decided that it was best if they went ahead with their vacation plans and not attend the funeral.

I remember sitting at the piano, playing for the funeral. As I
gazed into the audience, clearly one-half of the congregation was
my rather uptight family, and across the aisle the other half was
the most colorful collection of lipstick lesbians and gay men
you'd ever see. At one point before the service had started, my
cousin who went by the name "Uncle Beverly" as a waitress in a
gay bar in Provincetown entered the back of the chapel clad in
leather. Her throaty voice carried throughout the room as she
spewed, "My God, I've never seen so many fags in one room in
my life." Necks tightened and eyes widened on my family's side,
and there were scattered bursts of nervous, muffled laugher from
the other side. I played the piano just a little louder.

My aunt, Betty Lynne's mother, stared stoically forward during the service, seemingly scared that the lesbian energy in the
room might be catching. After the service, she refused to attend
the reception being held at Sylvia and Betty Lynne's beautiful
ocean-front home. She had never set foot in that den of iniquity,
and she wasn't about to now that the end had come.

I will never fully understand how a mother could keep herself from seeing, if for the last time, the life her daughter had created. For if she had, she would have seen a gathering of wonderful, educated women and men who loved her daughter dearly. She would have been forced to challenge her own tightly held belief that there was something sinister about a love between two women. And that just maybe her daughter had actually found the love she herself had never found in her own life, having divorced her husband in her mid-sixties after a long and tortured marriage.

The death of Betty Lynne was the death of hope for me. My family had little to do with me because I was gay, and I could only imagine that they would secretly whisper behind my back that HIV was God's punishment for being gay. It was a dark period, and honestly, I don't remember much about it other than being very discontent, an angry and emotionally shut-down lover, and deeply cynical. My partner at the time should be awarded sainthood for all that he put up with from me.

As the century changed, the landscape of lower Manhattan was scarred, the ire of the American public turned toward terrorism, and my life once again began a radical transformation. My relationship with my partner fell apart, and I found myself living in a small studio apartment in a charming but centuries-worn adobe building in the very heart of old Santa Fe. While not nearly as distraught as I had been when I walked away from my corporate career, I again found myself digging deep to find the passion I had on occasion tasted but never been able to hold in my life. I loved writing, but now I found myself with nothing inspired to write.

All throughout this journey, I continued to work more or less as a psychologist, and this above anything else brought me a quiet contentment. But now, after having followed my now ex-partner to Santa Fe, where his paintings sold to well-heeled tourists for a small fortune, I lived in a state where I had no license to practice as a psychotherapist. The road to gaining that license was particularly long and difficult, for New Mexico's regulations were designed to restrict an influx of out-of-state medical professionals. Living alone, struggling financially to make ends meet, I found myself working on the San Juan Pueblo, about an hour north of Santa Fe. Here I could gain the supervision I needed to meet the requirements of licensure as a psychologist, which would allow me to once again practice as a psychotherapist. I became the clinical director for a small drug-and-alcohol treatment facility called New Moon Lodge.

On my first day of work on the pueblo, I remember pulling up on the dirt road and parking in the dust-filled yard next to the mobile home that was my office. As I walked through the yard, my shiny black Prada shoes disappeared in the mounds of fine dust that seemed to cover everything in New Mexico. I cried without tears as I brushed aside the sad and toothless dog on the porch and opened the half-broken screen door that opened into a waiting room covered in worn carpet of a color that was virtually indistinguishable from the brownish-red dust from outside.

It was here, in this small mobile home in a forgotten Native American village on the shores of the Rio Grande, that I touched something I had always known but not always remembered. It was those moments of clarity that sometimes arose in sessions with clients where out of the pain of their anxiety and chaos, a newer understanding of the self emerged. I experienced moments of quiet joy and contentment seeing my clients grow and find relief from the weariness and pain that had plagued many of them since they were young children. It was the same experience

I had known while sitting bedside with AIDS patients a decade earlier. This time, however, I was different. The years of running from shame had changed and broken me, and this time I was determined to hold on to what I had found. At forty years old, I finally had some certainty about who I was and what I wanted in life. Hope was slowly returning.

Up to this point, my life had bounced between three failed relationships with life partners, numerous moves between cities, and persistent uncertainty about being a therapist, a business executive, a management consultant, and a writer. As I look back, I can see myself grasping for something of substance and meaning, but never really knowing what it was. I kept grasping, not realizing that the problem was inside me, as was the solution, and not in trying the next new job opportunity, city, or even handsome man that crossed my path. It wasn't until I was twenty years beyond the normal years of adolescence that I finally began to emerge as a man.

As I look back and try to describe for you what was so different for me now, it was finally accepting that joy in life comes not from our successes, but from how we live life. It isn't about those Prada shoes I was so proud of, or whether I worked in a posh Beverly Hills office or a run-down mobile home. Those things had very little to do with what makes me feel joy: The smile on the face of a mother who finally has her son back from the dark pit of heroin addiction or the couple that begins to see a way to reunite their love after betrayal and heartbreak when they never thought it possible. Walking my dog beside the ocean. The touch of a man who loves me honestly and whose face betrays the contents of his heart rather than just his physical beauty. The voice of a good friend when we haven't talked for days, or watching him belt out a show tune on YouTube. These things bring me joy and make me content.

In the years since those days on the pueblo, I have written more books and even become the CEO of a well-known residential treatment center, but through it all I remained focused on my quiet joy and never ventured too far in my career from the therapy room where two people meet to share a moment of authentic honesty and compassion. For me, it is my sanctuary and my joy. At times I have grown weary, but I have never tired of the therapeutic encounter. Here, in this place, is my passion.

So many gay men that I work with struggle, as I did, with being Peter Pan. They are talented, competent, and motivated, but they are also stuck in an emotional adolescence. They make money, create a beautiful life full of friends and lovers, and eat dessert as if it were the main course. Some are HIV-positive, but many are not. It seems that HIV, when it is present, often acts as a mere catalyst to the growing problem that is already within us.

My journey into manhood, while uniquely my own, turned out to not be all that different from every man's quest—straight or gay—to become an authentic man. What is common in my life with many other gay men is that the normal development into emotional manhood that should have happened during the second decade of life often doesn't happen until much later, if it happens at all. Many of us live in a delayed adolescence that persists for decades until we learn the critical skills that allow us to traverse the passages between adolescence and manhood.

The traumatic effect of growing up in a world where we must hide the truth of our strongest feelings causes our development to stall. We aren't able to have a normal adolescence where we experiment with who we are and receive the critical reflection of those around us that helps us to create a secure identity. Instead, we must hide, presenting to the world a fabricated version of ourselves until the day that we are free to express our sexuality and step out of the closet of shame. For so many of us, the experience of truly coming out comes too late, and the impact on our identity formation is profound. We are left floundering, with undeveloped internal guides that, should they have been allowed to develop, would have guided us toward discovering our passion and a stronger sense of ourselves.

It took the better part of two decades for the Peter Pan in me to grow up and become a man. During that time, there were fits and starts, progress and setbacks. The process of emotionally maturing—discovering the authentic nature of ourselves—happens slowly over time. It is an important process, however, if we are to ever experience lasting contentment in life. Contentment, it seems, is the one thing that remains just out of the reach of an adolescent.

There is one other insight that I learned along the way that has had an immeasurable impact on me. It is, quite simply, that my life changes as I practice certain skills I've learned that increase joy in my life. In other words, there's no big "ah-ha" moment, no must-read book, no teacher I must find. What makes a measurable difference in my life is when I practice—meaning "do"—certain things that are likely to improve my life and increase my contentment. Likewise, when I don't do these things (I like to call them "skills"), my inner peace and joy are diminished.

Many of the skills I have learned are not unique to me and have come to me from a variety of places. One of the more significant places where I learned these skills was in my own training in Dialectical Behavior Therapy (DBT). DBT taught me that love, joy, contentment, fulfillment, passion—virtually all the good things in life—come to us because we practice what we know works. The secret to life isn't an idea—it's a behavior. You must *do*, not just *think about*, what is likely to bring you joy and peace.

As I'm often asked by audiences, How does a gay man get to the place where he no longer struggles with compensation from shame and is able to live consistently in authenticity? It is here, in the learning and practicing of life-changing skills, that we are transformed from being emotional adolescents who struggle to find some lasting contentment into men who are grounded in themselves, at peace, and fulfilled.

Suffering isn't a precursor for change, despite what my own story may imply. My struggle brought me to a teachable moment in life where I could finally learn to practice skills that would improve my life. You don't have to take the same road. At any point that you are willing and ready to start practicing, you can begin. Each of us makes a choice in each moment how our lives will unfold. I invite you to consider making a change for the better.

Notes

CHAPTER 1

1. Ackerman, Robert. *Silent Sons: A Book for and About Men.* Fireside: New York, 1993, p. 101.

CHAPTER 5

1. Vidal, Gore. *Palimpsest.* Random House: New York, 1995, p. 24.

CHAPTER 11

1. Angelou, Maya. *A Song Flung Up to Heaven,* pp. 159–160.

CHAPTER 12

1. LeDoux, J.E., Romanski, L., Xagoraris, A. (1991). Indelibility of subcortical emotional memories. *Journal of Cognitive Neuroscience* 1:238–243.

2. Gurvits, T.G., Shenton, M.R., Hokama, H., Ohta, H., Lasko, N.B., Gilbertson, M.W., Orr, S.P., Kikinis, R., Jolesz, F.A., McCarley, R.W., & Pitman, R.K. (1996). Magnetic resonance imaging study of hippocampal volume in chronic, combat-related posttraumatic stress disorder. *Biological Psychiatry* 40:1091–1099.

Acknowledgments

Abby Braun, Ph.D.
Don & Eunice Downs
Marnie Cochran
Cedar Koons, LISW
Kristina Lindstrom
Donna McCoy, Ph.D.
Nesha Morse, Psy.D.
Santa Fe DBT Consultation Team
Susan Schulman
Steven Sugarman

A special thanks to all my clients who have been willing to share their lives with me. You are my greatest teachers.

Index